INVESTOPOLY

THE 8 GOLDEN RULES FOR MASTERING THE GAME OF BUILDING WEALTH

STUART WEMYSS

First published in 2018 by Major Street Publishing Pty Ltd
PO Box 106, Highett, Vic. 3190
E info@majorstreet.com.au
W majorstreet.com.au
M +61 421 707 983

Ordering information

Quantity sales. Special discounts are available on quantity purchases by corporations, associations and others. For details, contact Lesley Williams using the contact details above.

Individual sales. Major Street publications are available through most bookstores. They can also be ordered directly from Major Street's online bookstore at www.majorstreet.com.au/shop.

Orders for university textbook/course adoption use. For orders of this nature, please contact Lesley Williams using the contact details above.

A catalogue record for this
book is available from the
National Library of Australia

ISBN: 978-0-6482387-2-0

Internal design by Production Works
Cover design by Simone Geary
Printed in Australia by Griffin Press

10 9 8 7 6 5 4 3 2 1

Disclaimer: The material in this publication is of the nature of general comment only, and neither purports nor intends to be advice. Readers should not act on the basis of any matter in this publication without considering (and if appropriate taking) professional advice with due regard to their own particular circumstances. The author and publisher expressly disclaim all and any liability to any person, whether a purchaser of this publication or not, in respect of anything and the consequences of anything done or omitted to be done by any such person in reliance, whether whole or partial, upon the whole or any part of the contents of this publication.

CONTENTS

ABOUT THE AUTHOR

Stuart Wemyss is a qualified chartered accountant, independent financial advisor and mortgage broker with over 20 years' experience. He founded his business, ProSolution Private Clients, in 2002 and has helped hundreds of clients invest successfully. Stuart is licensed to provide financial, credit and tax advice, which means he is able to give holistic advice.

Stuart has always passionately believed in the need for people to be able to access a trustworthy source of independent financial advice. Nothing upsets him more than to hear about selfish advisors ripping off their unsuspecting clients! This passion is what drives him daily to write books and blogs, publish podcasts, appear in the media, advise his clients, mentor his staff and give presentations – whatever it takes to help more people access a source of unbiased information and advice.

Stuart is married, lives in Melbourne and has two children. He is a passionate Cats supporter (AFL) and loves a glass of wine (or three)!

If you would like to hear more from Stuart, you can subscribe to his blog and podcast at www.investopoly.com.au.

ACKNOWLEDGEMENTS

Many people have helped shape my experience, knowledge and views in investment markets over the past 20 years, all of whom have encouraged me to write this book.

Of course, my family and friends are always of great support. My wife has suffered my many long absences while toiling with this book – thank you.

I would also like to especially thank Paul Nugent and Richard Wakelin, who supported me when I started my business many years ago. And Joe Bongiorno has been very generous with his time and advice. Thank you gentlemen.

To all the team (past and present) at ProSolution Private Clients, thank you for pouring your heart into helping our clients each and every day. It's a pleasure to work with a group of people who passionately care for our clients' wellbeing.

This book is dedicated to
my beautiful wife who lights up my soul.
You give my life meaning and purpose.
I'd be lost without you.

HOW THIS BOOK IS DIFFERENT AND WHY IT MIGHT HELP YOU

As a financial advisor, when I meet people for the first time they tend to ask questions like the following:

- 'I know I need to do something, but where do I start?!'

- 'Should I focus on repaying my home loan as my top priority?'

- 'Do I need to invest in property as well as shares, contribute more into super or look at different options?'

No doubt you have similar questions (you're reading this introduction after all), and helping you answer questions like these is exactly why I've written this book. In it, I outline how you can plan your financial journey using a robust and proven investment framework: my eight golden rules to winning the 'game' of building personal wealth.

What financial steps you need to take next will only become clear when you understand how this game and its rules work.

Games are won by applying proven rules and strategies

You've likely noticed the title of this book is a play on the board game Monopoly – the ultimate trading game. Let's be honest, winning Monopoly requires a little bit of luck – for example, land-ing on unowned property and avoiding properties already owned by your opponent. But, in truth, the key to winning this game is making the most of your luck and applying certain rules – such as buying as much property as possible, not spending all your cash (having some savings) and negotiating to get a full set as soon as you can. Following these rules will see you winning more games of Monopoly than you lose (and perhaps flipping fewer boards over in frustration).

Building wealth is no different. You can win at the game of building personal wealth by applying a set of proven rules. These golden rules are all proven (they work) and are rooted in logic and simple maths – they are not my or anyone else's opinion and can be verified with historical evidence. These rules include things like have a plan, spend less than you earn, forget about the short term and always make decisions that maximise long-term wealth and, if you are going to invest in property, make sure it's 'investment-grade'.

Follow my eight fundamentally sound, easy-to-understand golden rules – it's that simple!

I believe that mapping out a financial plan so that you can have a safe and secure retirement is a lot easier than you might think. Understanding and consistently applying my golden rules will help you work out what you should do next (investment-wise), with virtually no chance of making a mistake – even if you don't have a 'financial brain'.

If you already use a financial advisor, the golden rules will help you work out if the advice you receive is sound. They will put you in control of your financial destiny.

Virtually all mistakes are predictable – my golden rules will filter out mistakes before they occur

Very few investment mistakes occur because of random bad luck, and virtually all investment mistakes are predictable. In other words, mistakes are caused by doing something fundamentally wrong.

I propose that if you test all your past and current investment decisions against the eight golden rules outlined in this book, you'll be able to highlight where you went right or wrong. More importantly, if you filter all future investment decisions through these eight golden rules, you'll be able to prevent all predictable mistakes. Applied consistently, these golden rules guarantee success (putting aside random bad luck, which rarely occurs).

This book is all about 'pure investment'

You can build personal wealth in three ways: by investing, speculating and business ownership. These three strategies are illustrated in the following figure.

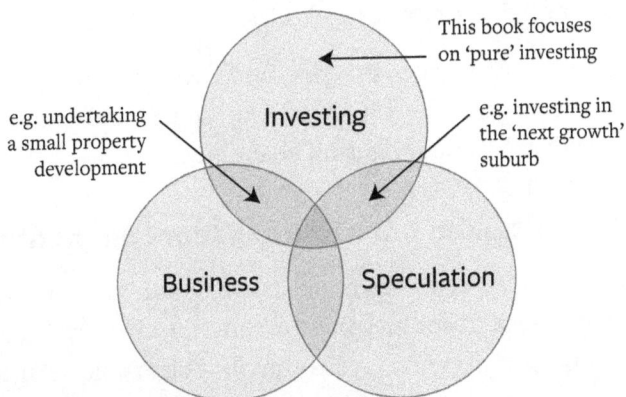

When trying to build wealth, you need to understand which of these strategies you're using (that is, investing, speculating or owning a business) because they each have very different risks and wildly different success rates.

You also need to be aware that you could be doing a bit of both. For example, investing in property in a location that is unproven but that you expect to 'take off' is closer to speculation, rather than investing. Many people may fool themselves into believing they are investing, but they are not.

To build wealth safely and successfully, you need to employ an easily repeatable strategy. Good investment strategies and methodologies generate ongoing investment returns, year on year, with virtually no input from you. However, in contrast, success in speculation and business is rarely repeatable without a lot of intellectual input from you. That is, you must keep discovering new ideas (for example, picking a new stock or new asset such as bitcoin, or predicting the next growth suburb or development site) each year to make money, which is very difficult to do consistently.

This book is about pure investment. Pure investing is all about generating the highest return for the absolute lowest risk, using proven, repeatable strategies and rules.

I outline my golden rules in more detail over the course of this book, showing you how simple it is to understand money and build wealth safely. But first, a bit about me ...

I'm a practitioner, not a journalist or commentator

I am a doer, not a teacher or commentator. This book consolidates my 21 years' experience as a financial advisor, chartered accountant, mortgage broker and investor into my eight golden rules.

If you want to build a house, would you prefer to engage a licensed builder with 30 years' experience on the tools or someone who is building their first home? We all make mistakes while we are learning our trade. The experienced builder probably made mistakes on the first few houses they built, and so had to go back and rectify them. After 30 years, you'd expect them to no longer make the same mistakes. The experienced builder has had to solve many problems and challenges over the 30 years. There probably aren't many challenges they haven't solved yet – they've seen it all.

I don't know of anyone who wouldn't say that they aren't a lot better at their job after 20 years of experience. Learning and doing are two very different things.

The golden rules contained in this book have been formulated and refined over my two decades of practice, observation and experience. They are not just theory. They have been tested and proven to work.

I have nothing to sell you

As mentioned, I'm a qualified and licensed chartered accountant, financial planner and mortgage broker. I am a registered tax agent and hold my own Australian Financial Services Licence and Australian Credit License. My 21 years' experience includes running my own financial advisory business in Melbourne – ProSolution Private Clients – for the last 16 years.

I do not make any money selling or recommending investments – and never will. Many property books are written by buyers' agents. Many share investing books are written by stock brokers and fund managers. This doesn't make them bad books. It just means that this book is different because I'm an independent umpire. I don't care if my clients invest in shares, property, bonds or whatever – because I have no vested interest. My only interest is that they invest in what is appropriate and helps them achieve their goals.

I would love to hear your feedback...

If you enjoy this book, please share it with the people you care about. If you love it, I would greatly appreciate it if you spent a few minutes to share your review on Amazon or Google. Doing so will help people better understand how this book may help them.

Finally, throughout the book I direct you to www.investopoly. com.au to download additional materials at no cost. Here you can also subscribe to my weekly blog.

As we launch into my golden rules and how you can apply them to your financial situation, I wish you the best success with your investing.

PLAY THE LONG GAME

In this chapter, I discuss why taking a long-term approach with almost all financial decisions is critical. I outline why the best quality financial decisions are almost always long-term ones, and why short-term profit does not create long-term value for anyone. In short, this chapter demonstrates why you will ultimately become an unsuccessful investor by thinking short-term, and being impatient and greedy.

Delayed gratification is your best friend – and an indicator of success

Delayed gratification is the conscious decision to direct money in a manner that will not enhance your lifestyle in the short term (in fact, it might have a negative impact on your lifestyle right now), but will substantially improve your financial position and lifestyle in the long run.

Delayed gratification has been proven to provide improvements in many parts of life, including finances. A famous longitudinal study on the impact of delayed gratification – called the 'marshmallow test' – was conducted by Professor Walter Mischel at Stanford University in the 1960s. The test involved offering preschoolers the option of one marshmallow now or, if they waited approximately 15 minutes, two marshmallows (during which time the tester left the room). Several follow-up studies were completed years later in the 1980s and 1990s, and these found that the children who exhibited a capacity for delayed gratification went on to have higher educational achievement, a higher sense of self-worth and a better ability to cope with stress.

Let's look at a real-life example. Ben is a 30-year-old project manager. He has just received a $15,000 p.a. pay rise. Ben is faced with two decisions. He can upgrade his car and spend approximately $9000 on a car lease (which is the equivalent to his after-tax increase in income – that is, $15,000 minus $6000 in tax). Or he can invest this extra income with some borrowings – that is, invest $750 per month in cash plus $750 per month from borrowings (making a total investment of $1500 per month) into a diversified low-cost share market investment. In my experience, people tend to get used to a certain standard of living and rarely make voluntarily decisions that will result in a 'downgrade' to their standard of living. As such, if Ben chooses the first option, it is reasonable to assume that he will continue to spend $9000 p.a. on a car lease for the long run (because he'd continue to update his car at the end of each lease period).

In ten years' time, if Ben chose to invest, he would conservatively have $159,000 in equity in his share market investments (and this would snowball to over $550,000 in 20 years' time – assuming a 5 per cent p.a. dividend yield plus 5 per cent p.a. growth).

Alternatively, if Ben had the capacity to borrow more, he could use the $15,000 of pre-tax income to fund the cash flow shortfall of a $400,000 investment-grade property. In ten years' time following this option, Ben would have over $350,000 of equity in that property (and over $1 million in 20 years' time – assuming a 7 per cent p.a. growth rate plus 3 per cent p.a. gross rental yield). Of course, if Ben chose the car, his financial position would not have improved.

Understanding that a significant long-term reward comes from making long-dated financial decisions is very important. Most people don't appreciate how significant the differences are in financial terms. Think back over your life. Did you make decisions 5, 10 or 20 years ago that continue to affect your finances now? Would taking a different path have resulted in a significantly improved financial position?

Of course, I am not suggesting that every decision we make should only consider the financial implications. Lifestyle considerations are important and it's imperative to enjoy the journey rather sacrificing everything until you reach your destination (that is, financial independence). I think the key word here is 'balance'. For more on this, see Golden Rule #3.

The perils of short-term thinking

Short-term thinking isn't just dangerous when thinking about your lifestyle versus investment choices. When you have decided to invest, a short-term outlook often creates a lot of anxiety about possible changes in the market. What if the market drops 5 per cent next week? What if the property market bubble bursts? And so on. Fear causes people to worry about investing in an asset one day, only for its price to plummet the following day, week or month. This fear often results in paralysis – that is, when faced with a risky decision, it's far easier for humans to do nothing at all. Conversely, if we take a long-term approach (for example, you ask yourself which stock or property you can invest in today that will be worth four times its current value in 20 years' time), any short-term market price volatility is put into perspective and becomes largely inconsequential. This is the best way to quell any anxiety that you might have about making investment decisions.

Howard Schultz, the man who built the $100 billion Starbucks behemoth, once said in an interview with Oprah Winfrey that 'short-term profit does not create long-term value for anyone'. This is a very profound and important point when it comes to investing. Take stock picking as an example. Let's say that I have a crystal ball and I can pick a stock that's going to perform very well over the next two years, meaning I can invest in that stock and enjoy the returns. However, in two years' time, I must find the 'next winner'. And then again two years after that. And again, and again. Putting aside the fact that it is near on impossible to pick winning stocks consistently year after year after year (more on this in Golden Rule #4), this is not a strategy that generates long-term value. We can all choose from many investment strategies. My proposition is that you should select the ones that are focused on generating long-term value, because they have a significantly higher probability of working.

Markets are not efficient in the short-run – so invest accordingly

The efficient-market hypothesis – formulated by economist Eugene Fama – essentially states that stocks always trade at their fair market value. I think this theory is broadly correct in the long run, but also believe, in the short run, markets are often affected by irrational levels of confidence and pessimism. If you invest in the stock market today and intend to hold that investment for at least the next 10 years, I don't think you need to worry too much about the impact of irrational human behaviour. However, if you take a short-term approach towards investing, this irrational behaviour is another thing you probably should worry about.

Let's look at another example. In October 2007, the S&P 500 index (the best gauge of the US large-cap share market) was trading at over 1500 points. By March 2009, it had lost more than half its value and fallen to below 700 points. At the time of writing, the S&P 500 is trading at above 2,600 points which equates to an average capital return (excluding dividend income) of over 5.5 per cent p.a. over a 10-year period that included a massive stock market crash – that's not too bad, considering! If your investment approach is fundamentally sound, then 'time heals all wounds'.

The Australian property market is less susceptible to irrational behaviour because high entry (stamp duty) and exit (agent selling fees) costs render it uneconomical to speculate. However, the property market is made up of literally thousands of small geographical submarkets that are affected by their own idiosyncratic supply and demand factors. Due to this, irrational pricing of property can occur in these submarkets. A recent and excellent example of this was the property markets in mining towns. At the peak of the mining boom in 2012, a four-bedroom house in Moranbah, Queensland, sold for $850,000. In December 2016, that same house resold for only $300,000, crystallising an estimated loss of $590,000 including costs. Thousands more examples like this one can be found. People who invested in mining towns were encouraged by the prospect of short-term profit but, as Howard Schultz intimated, this came at the cost of long-term value.

In summary, we can't predict what markets will do in the short term. If you believe this to be true, the only solution is to take a long-term approach.

If I take a long-term approach, what investment returns can I expect?

I prefer to assess market returns over the long term – that is, over 20 to 30 years. Doing so means the assessment period includes various political environments, different economic growth periods, numerous interest rate cycles, and changes in law and taxation. The returns from the major growth asset classes of property and Australian and international shares do not vary that much over these longer terms – over the past 25 to 30 years, for example, total returns for these main asset classes ranged from 9.30 per cent to 12.0 per cent p.a. This highlights you can build wealth using any or all of these asset classes so long as you use the correct methodologies (which are outlined in this book). Which asset class you select depends on your situation and goals. The following sections look in more detail at the long-term returns from the major asset classes in Australia, starting with the Australian stock market.

Australian stock market 25-year returns

The following chart sets out the S&P/ASX 200 Total Return Index over the past 25 years. This index includes the top 200 Australian listed companies on the ASX and so represents approximately 80 per cent of the total Australian market (by market capitalisation). The Total Return Index also includes the impact of capital growth and dividends (reinvested). The growth in the S&P/ASX 200 Total Return Index (from 5920 in 1992 to 56,609 by October 2017) equates to a 9.3 per cent p.a. total return over the past 25 years.

S&P/ASX 200 Total Return Index from 1992 to 2017

Data source: www.marketindex.com.au

Australian property market 30-year returns

The next chart overleaf sets out the average median house price for Melbourne and Sydney over the 30 years since June 1987. The average capital growth rate over this period was 7.86 per cent p.a., with the average rental yield for houses in Melbourne and Sydney over the same period being 4.19 per cent p.a. Therefore, the overall return for these markets was just over 12 per cent p.a. over the past 30 years. As you may be aware, rental yields are greatly affected by interest rates (because when rates are high, it's cheaper to rent than own and vice versa). This means they have been sitting between 2.5 per cent and 3.5 per cent since approximately 2002. Based on this data, I think it's reasonable to expect an annual capital growth rate in the range of 7 to 9 per cent over the long term and a rental yield of 2 per cent to 3 per cent p.a. if you invest in investment-grade property (see Golden Rule #8 for more on what 'investment-grade' means).

Average median house price in Melbourne and Sydney/ Average rental yield

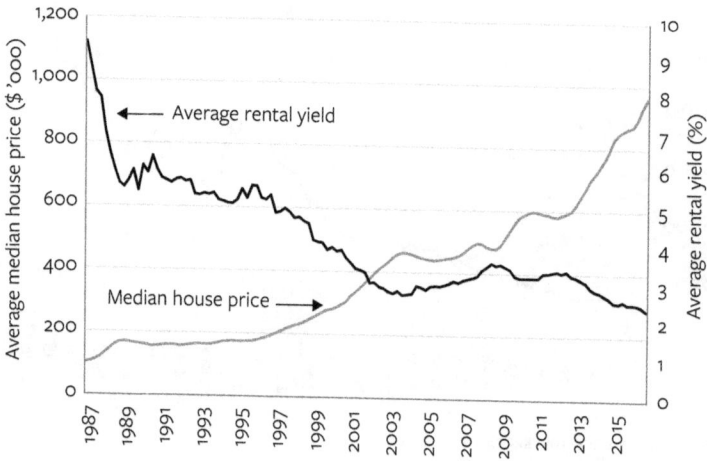

Data source: REIA

US stock market 30-year return

The chart opposite sets out the S&P 500 Total Return Index over the past 30 years. This index includes the top 500 companies listed on the New York Stock Exchange and NASDAQ by market value and accounts for approximately 80 per cent of the total market. The Total Return Index includes the impact of capital growth and dividend income (reinvested).

I have selected the S&P index because it's a broad-based index that, in my opinion, best represents the US market. In addition, the US market accounts for 54 per cent of the MSCI World Index. The second most dominant country/region is Europe, excluding the UK which accounts for 14 per cent. As you can see, the US market is a reasonable proxy for international markets.

The growth in the S&P 500 Total Return Index (from 256 in 1988 to 5150 by December 2017) equates to a 10.5 per cent p.a. total return over the past 30 years.

S&P 500 Total Return Index (US) from 1987 to 2017

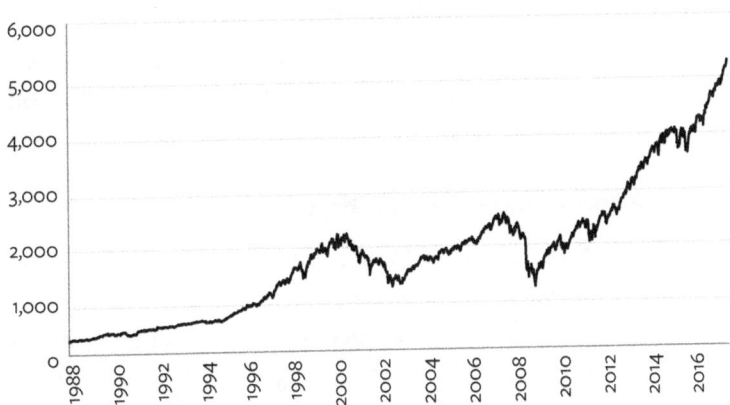

Data source: www.finance.yahoo.com

Comparing markets

The assessment provided in the preceding sections shows that the total market returns for shares versus property over the long run are not massively different from each other. (One important factor to consider is that the split of income and capital is quite different between these asset classes. I discuss this further in Golden Rule #5.)

Based on these market returns, taking a long-term approach means you can expect an investment return of approximately 10 per cent p.a. if you invest in any of these assets classes. With the correct investment strategy, these returns will be sufficient for most investors to achieve their goals – and if you're hoping for materially higher longer term returns than this, I suggest you probably need to adjust your expectations.

As discussed in the introduction to this book, a big difference exists between speculation and investing. If you can obtain a long-term return of 10 per cent p.a., why would you ever need to speculate?

The only answers I can think of are that you are impatient or greedy or both. Or you feel it's a more exciting approach that, if it works, will make you feel smarter than the average investor. All these reasons are flawed in my opinion and you are better off sticking to what works.

When is it appropriate to think short term?

In some situations, it may be appropriate to take a shorter term approach. These situations will more likely relate to 'timing' decisions rather than asset-selection decisions – for example, where your financial situation might be changing in the near future because your employment income is either increasing or decreasing. In this situation, of course it is important to take these events into account. That said, such decisions must still be made in the context of having a longer term strategy.

What is the best question you can ask yourself today?

As world-renowned author Jim Collins says, great questions are better than great answers. I believe the single best question you can ask yourself is 'What investment decision can I make today that with dramatically strengthen my financial position in 10 to 20 years?' The answer to this question often yields the highest quality answer from an investment perspective. And if you ask yourself that question regularly and act accordingly, it won't be long before you are well on the way to achieving financial independence.

Golden Rule #1 Summary

Here are the main points we've covered in this chapter:

- Greed and impatience entice us to think short term. This might generate short-term profit but rarely results in the accumulation of long-term value – because short-term, greedy thinking seduces you into adopting fundamentally flawed investment strategies.

- Thinking short term when investing fuels anxiety because you end up worrying about short-term market movements. This either results in you making emotionally charged financial decisions (which almost always result in mistakes) or paralysis – that is, the inability to make any decisions.

- No-one has a crystal ball, and no-one has developed a reliable and proven methodology for predicting which asset class will perform best in the short term. No-one knows what's going to happen in the short term so give up trying to predict it and focus on maximising your long-term outcomes.

- Long-term returns produced by the major asset classes are healthy enough for you to be able to fund retirement. Therefore, it's not which asset class you choose or when you invest that determines how successful you'll be – it's how you invest that counts. Focus on your methodology (which I cover in Golden Rules #7 and #8) and stick with that investment for the long term.

Now that you understand how important it is to think long term, let's talk about the next golden rule – which is making sure you have a clear goal, and a clear destination. Many people make the mistake of investing aimlessly and this results in them investing in the wrong assets and in the wrong order – thereby compromising their success. The next golden rule will save you from making the same mistakes.

KNOW HOW MUCH INCOME YOU NEED AND BY WHEN

Formulating even a basic financial plan is impossible without an idea of what you what to achieve and by when. Not starting with a goal (no matter how simple) is like jumping into your car and driving around without a destination. Having a goal gives you a context to make financial decisions – you can ask yourself, 'Out of *x* or *y*, which one will get me closer to my goal?' In the absence of a clear goal, deciding which option (that is, *x* or *y*) is best for you becomes very difficult.

This chapter highlights a number of important considerations when setting your financial goals. Remember – any goals are better than none, so do not feel as if you must be very detailed right from the start. Goals can (and will) be refined and clarified over time. By the end of this chapter, however, you will know which two goals you need to set and how to set them.

You don't need a map until you have a destination

Strategy before tactics. Always!

When you jump into your car to drive somewhere, you can easily work out the best route to get where you are going because you know the address of your destination. Imagine jumping into your car and driving around without a destination. You would just drive around aimlessly and achieve nothing.

Investing is no different. To invest without having a destination in mind (even if it's vague) is a complete waste of time – just like driving around aimlessly.

Should you invest in property? Invest in shares? Or repay your home loan? All of these options can be great wealth accumulation strategies but who knows which one is the most appropriate for you if we don't know your goal? It's a little bit like asking a personal trainer what's the best exercise you can do. It depends on what you want to achieve – for example, do you want to build muscle, lose weight or improve your aerobic fitness? This is why strategy always comes before tactics. Tactics refers to what to invest in whereas strategy refers to how to invest.

A very common mistake that many people make is thinking about tactics before they have a clear and simple investment strategy. The benefits of having a strategy in place will help ensure that your chosen tactics will achieve your goals in the most efficient manner (optimising for tax, interest, fees and so on).

More importantly, having a strategy will help ensure you don't waste any time heading down the wrong tunnel – and wasting time is the costliest mistake that an investor can make. As Warren Buffett says, 'No matter how great the talent or efforts, some things just take time. You can't produce a baby in one month by getting nine women pregnant!' There are no shortcuts. Building wealth requires much time and patience. So, start as soon as possible and make sure you are on the right path. And if you find yourself in a hole (or on the wrong path), stop digging.

So please, please do not invest in anything until you have set some clear and measurable financial goals. As I've already mentioned, your goals don't have to be detailed – they can be as simple as build wealth so that you have the ability to not work beyond age 60. Something is better than nothing.

Before we talk about how to set your retirement goals, however, let me discuss a few important considerations.

Retirement is an 'old fashioned' concept

Many people I talk with do not necessarily want to stop working completely. Instead, they would like to get themselves into a financial position that allows them to spend more time with family and pursuing their interests. For example, instead of aiming for full retirement at age 60, they might like to reduce their working hours to, say, three days per week and continue at that pace for a further 5 to 10 years.

However, if you do want to aim for full retirement by a certain age, having a think about what you will do with your time is very wise.

You may have heard the saying that the two most dangerous years in your life are the first year after you are born and the first year of retirement. According to 2013 research published by the Institute of Economic Affairs in the UK, for example, retirement increases your risk of clinical depression by 40 per cent.

World-renowned life coach Anthony Robbins suggests we all have six human needs (which he has formulated using Abraham Maslow's hierarchy of needs from 1943). These six needs are:

1. *Certainty* – the need to feel safe and in control

2. *Variety* – the enjoyment of some surprises

3. *Significance* – the need to feel important, special, unique or needed

4. *Love and connection* – to give and receive love

5. *Growth* – if you are not growing, you are dying

6. *Contribution* – meaning comes from what you give, not what you get; as Robbins says, 'living is giving'.

Robbins's theory is that if you can fulfil all of these six human needs, you will ultimately achieve happiness and fulfilment in life – meeting the first four, more basic needs will create happiness, while meeting the last two needs creates fulfilment. For most people, paid employment often contributes to needs five and six. Therefore, if you plan to stop working, you need to think about how you will continue to 'grow' (that is, learn and challenge yourself) and 'contribute' to others – and you should plan this well in advance of retirement. Some solutions can include alternative paid part-time employment, voluntarily work and becoming involved with community groups.

The reason I mention this is because I believe that people dramatically under-prepare for retirement – not only financially but also psychologically. For many people, ceasing paid employment might not actually be the most sensible option. Reducing working hours and/or changing occupation might be a much better solution – not only will it contribute to your finances, but it might result in a happier retirement experience for you and your partner.

My personal philosophy is never to retire. I cannot imagine a time where I will ever want to permanently stop working (subject to my health, of course). Instead, when I turned 40 I reduced my work week to four days to allow me more time for the other things I enjoy. I will no doubt reduce that to three days as I approach 50 years of age and then eventually to two days per week for as long as my health will allow it. I have heard that the former Victorian premier Jeff Kennett has suggested that a perfect retirement balance (for him) includes two days per week for paid employment, two days for community involvement and one day of personal relaxation. This sounds pretty good to me.

Of course, 'retirement' will be different for everyone. My only suggestion here is that you don't necessarily have to think of retirement as being a complete cessation of paid employment.

I don't care what my husband does in retirement as long as he doesn't do it at home.

Unknown

What if you don't die (until you're much older)?

Current life expectancy tables suggest that (statistically), as a 43-year-old male, I can expect to live to approximately 82 years of age. Of course, this is based on historical data and doesn't take into account my personal circumstances or what the future might hold. These tables do provide some context, however. A child born in 1914, for example, had a 1 per cent chance of making it to 100. For those born in 2014, that figure is now a 50 per cent chance.[1]

More so than ever before, accurately predicting our own life expectancy is difficult, because it will inevitably be affected by medical technologies and treatments that haven't even been discovered yet.

For example, IBM's artificial intelligence supercomputer, Watson, is now being used by doctors to develop treatment plans for cancer patients. Watson ingested 25 million Medline abstracts, over 1 million medical journal articles, data from 4 million patients and every drug patent since 1861 and can then use all this data to make recommendations and treatment plans. Watson can complete work that would take teams of specialist doctors many decades in a matter of hours. Indeed, IBM predicts that Watson will generate $US10 billion in revenue by 2024, and a big part of this will come from its use in medicine.

Moore's Law is the prediction that the power of a computer chip will double every two years while the cost to produce that chip will halve – a prediction made 40 years ago that has turned out to become true. In 2017, US tech billionaire Mark Cuban predicted that technology will advance more in the next decade than it did in the last three.

All of these advances will undoubtedly mean we live longer. You need to consider two important aspects as a result of this:

1. When planning your investment strategy, you need to ensure you have enough money to afford to live well into your nineties and perhaps beyond. In other words, you need to plan for what is referred to as 'survivorship risk' – the risk of living too long and running out of money.

2. You need to focus on investing in the right mix of assets so that your net worth continues to grow into retirement – otherwise known as the Holy Grail of retirement planning. This means that you are not eating into your capital to fund your living expenses. To do this you need an efficient mixture of growth and income assets (see Golden Rules #4 and #5 for more on this). If you achieve this, your survivorship risk is significantly reduced.

The other thing you need to think about is the cost of aged care. At some point you and/or your spouse might have to move into an aged-care facility. The demand for aged care in Australia is predicted to increase at a rate of 5 per cent p.a., and the cost to the federal government is expected to double over the next decade. This means that it will be more difficult and costly for self-funded retirees to afford quality accommodation. Today, a decent aged-care facility costs in the range of $250,000 to $350,000 (depending upon location). You may want to provide for this in your strategy. The best way to do this is to ensure that your net worth continues to appreciate well into retirement – and, again, you're on your way to achieving this if you follow the golden rules contained in this book.

The $100,000 p.a. income myth

When I ask people what annual income they would like in retirement, most say around $100,000 (after tax). However, very little science is often behind the answer – most people pluck this figure out of thin air. While it is true that aiming at something is better than nothing, developing a more considered income target is definitely worth the small investment of time required.

As a general rule, in my experience, a typical middle-class couple would spend in the range of $60,000 to $100,000 per year on general living expenses. This amount does not make any allowance for any substantial travel (such as overseas holidays) or expensive hobbies. However, please don't be swayed by this information. Your number is your number. If you are going to the trouble of developing a strategy (and reading this book), you should make sure that your investment strategy will help you achieve something that is meaningful to you. A retirement income goal is a very personal thing. Picking someone else's goal simply to save time might end up being a big mistake. In the following sections, I help you work out a retirement income goal that's right for you and your situation.

Working out what income you might need in retirement

It is difficult to make predictions, especially about the future
Danish proverb

The further away you are from retirement, the more inherently difficult it is to predict what income you will need to enjoy a comfortable retirement lifestyle. And regardless of the time left to retirement, it's inevitable that your wants and desires will change between now and then. But that doesn't mean you give up. Aiming at something is always better than aiming at nothing. And don't be shy. Be ambitious – these are goals, after all.

A good starting point is to work out what you spend at the moment on general living expenses. The next Golden Rule provides much more detail on how to work this out. For now, know that general living expenses include all expenses except mortgage repayments, children's education and large discretionary expenditure such as European holidays. They do include everything you need to spend to enjoy a comfortable lifestyle – including money spent on utilities, food, health, insurance, entertainment and clothes.

Once you have worked out what you spend now on expenses, you need to make nominal adjustments for those expenses that won't persist in retirement (typically expenses relating to looking after children and employment – for example, travel costs related to getting to and from work). Also, you will need to make allowances for new or higher expenses in retirement – such as those related to holidays (try to strike a yearly average), hobbies, medical expenses (due to medications and more frequent visits to the doctor) and any other planned or foreseen activities.

Another thing you should consider is where you will live. Will you still occupy your current home, or will it be too large (and too much to maintain) in retirement? Would you like to move out of the city and perhaps have a property in the country, or one near the beach plus a city apartment? I have two comments to add about this:

1. Some people think they might crystallise some equity when they sell and downsize their home, and so count on that equity to partly fund retirement. I advise avoiding doing that. Most people get used to living in a certain area that offers certain amenities. Often their friends live in the same area too. So, while they might eventually downsize in terms of accommodation size, they may not crystallise a lot of equity – they may, for example, sell the family home and buy a well-located townhouse in the same area. These properties might well be of similar values. A home is a personal use asset. It's not an investment asset (purchased with the sole purpose of funding retirement). Therefore, don't rely on crystallising equity as part of your retirement strategy. If it happens, it's icing on the cake.

2. If you do plan on downsizing *and* if your existing property is in a location that is likely to appreciate in price (between now and when you retire), building that into your strategy might be worthwhile.

Let me share an example on my second point with you. I have some clients whose owner-occupied property is in a blue-chip location. This property is worth over $1.5 million (with no debt) and, all things remaining equal, we expect the property's future capital growth prospects to be very strong. The couple expect to retire in approximately seven years. When they retire, they would like to have a small property in the country where they will spend most of their time (they'll need to spend about $500,000 on this) and a small unit in the city (around a $650,000 purchase). Because of the value of their home and their desires, it is pretty obvious that they will crystallise some equity from their home when they retire.

However, we want to delay selling their home for as long as possible so that they enjoy as much (tax-free) capital growth as possible. After much discussion and analysis, we decided the best strategy for them was to purchase an investment-grade unit (refer to Golden Rule #7) now. This will achieve two things:

1. Purchasing now will guard against the risk that the price of the unit will be a lot more expensive in seven years' time (meaning the purchase would eat into their equity).

2. The property will act as a safety net in case their super doesn't perform as well as expected.

Their retirement will be largely funded by their super and the equity they will crystallise from their home. On paper, this is a substantial amount. However, if something were to go wrong, they now have an investment-grade unit that they can either rent out or sell. It's a sort of 'plan B'. I always like to plan for the worse but hope for the best. Always thinking about 'what could go wrong' and putting plans in place to mitigate those risks now (before they eventuate) results in a robust and lower-risk investment strategy.

One final word of warning is to avoid relying on the assumption that you will generate employment income beyond age 65. I know that earlier in this chapter I discussed continuing to work can be a good strategy (for mental health). However, I am very reluctant to develop a strategy for a client that assumes they will still be receiving income from work beyond age 65. The reason is simply health might not allow it. You are better off being conservative with your assumptions and being delighted on the upside – rather than being caught out.

Take some time now with your spouse to think about all these issues. Discuss what each of you might like in retirement – including how you plan on spending your time. You might not 'know' what you want at this stage. Instead, look at this process as kind of like a wish list. Dream what you would like. This is an investment strategy. The whole point of this exercise is to work out what you need to do over the next decade/s to achieve your dreams. Like I said earlier, don't be afraid to be aspirational. With the correct approach (that is, following the eight golden rules in this book) and a reasonable amount of time, you can achieve some amazing financial outcomes.

Two critical 'must-have' goals

While you can have any number of lifestyle and financial goals, you need only two financial goals as a minimum:

1. You must know how much money you will need in retirement. If you have no idea, the best number to use is what you are currently spending (which we'll look at in the next chapter).

2. You must know when you would like to retire (that is, the age when you would like to have the choice of whether to work or not). Most of my clients aim for 60 years of age.

Realise that your goals will probably change

If retirement is more than a decade away, your preferences will very likely change by the time you reach retirement age – and so you need to revisit this planning process every one to two years. As time passes and retirement moves closer, your goals and dreams will probably become clearer and more definitive. The most important thing is to ask yourself these questions regularly:

1. Where am I heading? What does my life in retirement look like?

2. Given my answers to question 1, what can I do today to ensure that I am positioned financially to make these dreams a reality?

Don't force the answer to these questions. If nothing comes to mind immediately, continue with your existing goals and plan, no matter how vague they are. When you are ready for it, your goals will come to you. Just keep asking yourself these questions.

Planning beyond yourself

Some people have goals and desires that extend beyond their own retirement and include things like funding their grandchildren's private education, helping their children purchase their first property or supporting charities.

The best way to accommodate these goals is to look after yourself – that is, invest today in a way that maximises your long-term financial outcomes. If you follow my eight golden rules, in time, you will build substantial wealth. And when you are in a very strong financial position, lots of options will be available to you to help the people your love and organisations you care about.

Goals such as helping your children buy their first property are difficult to plan for because you:

*   don't know when you might want to provide this assistance
*   also don't know in what form the assistance might be – for example, as a cash gift or a family guarantee (more information following these points)

- may not even need or want to provide any assistance when the time comes to it – especially if the child is terrible at managing money and/or is uninterested in buying a property.

In reality, for the vast majority of parents, the best way to help your children buy a property is to provide what's called a 'family guarantee'. A family guarantee essentially allows your child to use some of the equity in your property to secure their loan. The deposit requirements are usually the most difficult to achieve (save) for first home buyers, so this option means they don't need to save as much for a deposit. To be able to provide a family guarantee, all you need to have is a property with plenty of equity (equity is the difference between the property's value and the loan amount). This demonstrates that if all you do is worry about yourself (that is, build wealth for yourself), you will also very likely be in a position to help others in the future too.

If you do have some very defined plans to help other people and your retirement is already provided for financially, you should seek independent financial advice (see the final chapter in this book) because using certain investment vehicles to achieve this (such as discretionary trusts) might be advantageous. You also need to ensure your estate plan (wills and so on) adequately accommodates these goals.

Golden Rule # 2 summary

In this chapter, we have discussed:

- You need to start with the end in mind. If you aim for nothing that is exactly what you will achieve. Setting clear financial goals is important because doing so provides a context for deciding what to invest in, how much and when. It also forces you to work out if your strategy will actually help you achieve your goals or not. This will make sure you don't waste precious time pursuing the wrong strategy.

- People are increasingly realising that their preference is for a phased retirement – that is, reducing working hours rather than ceasing work altogether. The best thing to do is develop an investment strategy that will allow you to retire in full. Then, if you have a desire to continue working and your health allows it, whether you continue to work is entirely your prerogative.

- You need to take into account your 'survivorship risk' of outliving your money. Most people should plan on funding living expenses well into their nineties.

- You absolutely must set two goals: how much income you need to fund a comfortable retirement and when (what age) you want to retire. If you don't know how much money you will need, use what you are spending today (and see the next chapter for help confirming this). And if you are struggling to set a retirement age, aim for somewhere between 60 and 65.

- Try to avoid relying on crystallising equity in your home to fund retirement (when you eventually sell it). The best thing to do is ignore any home equity.

- Revisiting these goals every one to two years is wise. This helps to ensure they are still appropriate and realistic.

Cash flow management is absolutely critical for wealth accumulation. You must spend less than you earn and invest the difference with regular discipline. In the golden rule, I show you how to do this without turning into a scrooge.

---

1 Figures taken from *The 100-Year Life: Living and Working in an Age of Longevity*, by Lynda Gratton and Andrew Scott, published in 2016

GOLDEN RULE #3

SPEND LESS THAN YOU EARN AND INVEST THE DIFFERENCE REGULARLY

Building wealth is simple: spend less than you earn and invest the difference regularly. It's a simple strategy and it works.

If you spend all your income – or worse, more than your income – you're unlikely to ever become financially independent. If you're a 'spender', this might sound like bad news. However, don't despair. You might be able to have your cake and eat it too.

This chapter sets out what you need to do to adequately manage your cash flow – including how to budget, how to become a better saver and how to reign in expenditure without dramatically impacting your lifestyle.

Master your cash flow: It's not what you earn but what you spend that counts

I have plenty of clients on modest incomes who have accumulated substantial wealth. Conversely, I have clients who have seven-figure incomes who have relatively few assets to show for it. You don't have to earn a massive income to become independently wealthy – although it certainly helps, it's not a prerequisite. The size of your surplus income is what counts. A huge salary is worthless if you spend it all and have nothing left at the end of the month.

Surplus income is how much money you have left over each week, fortnight or month after you pay for all living expenses and financial commitments. The larger your surplus income, the more successful you can be at building wealth.

Would you like to be paid now and in retirement?

You go to work and get paid a certain amount per week, fortnight or month. If you spend all that money now (and don't invest any of it), you only get paid once. Once it's gone, it's gone. However, you can effectively be paid twice. If you invest a portion of your income now, with time and patience (and if you follow the golden rules in this book), this money will generate a healthy amount of income and capital growth so that you can get paid again in retirement – maybe even multiple times if you are lucky. Sounds good, doesn't it?

So why don't more people follow this strategy? Because it requires delayed gratification. As discussed in Golden Rule #1, delayed gratification is the act of foregoing enjoyment now, in return for generating more enjoyment later.

How can you train yourself to become better at delayed gratification?

When does an investor make money? When they make (buy) the investment? Or when they sell the investment (or receive some of the returns)? I would argue that an investor makes money through the act of investing – it's just that the investment returns haven't revealed themselves yet. It's like when you plant seeds in your veggie garden. Most of the hard work is done. Apart from some watering and checking for pests, you just have to wait for the time it takes for your crop to grow before you can harvest and enjoy the fruits of your labour. Investing is no different.

Therefore, the best way to deal with the pains of delayed gratification is to tell yourself a different story. Don't tell yourself that you can't go on a holiday this year because you promised yourself that you would invest a minimum of $10,000 per year. Tell yourself that saving $10,000 this year will increase your net worth by $105,000 (in today's dollars) in 20 years' time (assuming modest returns) – and that's a smart investment. What would you prefer: $10,000 now or $105,000 later (which is circa $170,000 in future dollars)? Whatever you save today, you will get back 10 times more in value in 20 years' time.

How did I work this out? Well, if you buy a $650,000 investment property today and borrow the full cost, the after-tax negative cash flow to hold this investment over a 20-year period (including all costs such as interest at 7 per cent p.a. minus rental income and tax savings) is conservatively $120,000. Therefore, $10,000 pays for approximately 8.3 per cent of this negative cash flow (8.3 per cent of $120,000 is $10,000). And 8.3 per cent of the projected equity in the property in 20 years' time is $105,000 in today's dollars (assuming a 7.5 per cent p.a. growth rate). By saving $10,000 this year, you are 8.3 per cent closer to realising this equity. This is a far better story to tell yourself than focusing on the missed holiday. Or you can tell yourself that you are, say, 5 per cent closer to retirement.

The goal is happiness, not pleasure

Understand that the act of investing is what will help you become independently wealthy. Tell yourself that smart and successful people invest regularly, and you are one of them. Feel empowered by the fact that short-term rewards don't generate long-term satisfaction (plenty of studies have shown that the satisfaction gained from buying a new pair of shoes or a bottle of wine is always short-lived). That's the difference between happiness and pleasure – pleasure is always short-lived. You can't control the world around you. You can only control the story you tell yourself about the world around you, your money and what you do with it. And the best way to control your money and your spending is through budgeting.

What is budgeting?

Budgeting gets a bad rap. Many people view budgeting as something that's going to restrict their lifestyle enjoyment and spontaneity – but it's just not true. Budgeting is simply knowing where your money is going. As the saying goes, you can't manage what you don't measure. If you don't know where your money is going, how do you know if it's being spent efficiently?

If you want to spend $200 per week on eating out and this gives you a lot of satisfaction, do it. That is very different to spending $100 per month on Foxtel even though you almost never watch TV. To allocate your expenditure to achieve the highest levels of pleasure, you first need to know where all your money is going. This is the act of budgeting – that is, tracking expenditure.

Why most people don't budget

When I meet a prospective client, I always ask them what they spend on general living expenses. Approximately 19 out of 20 people don't know the answer to this question! Even if you're not interested in building wealth, surely you want to ensure your hard-earned money is being spent wisely – that is, that you're achieving maximum pleasure per dollar – don't you?

When I ask clients to review their expenditure, they commonly find they're spending money on things that really don't improve their enjoyment in life. They quickly realise they can eliminate these expenses without ever regretting their decision or missing these items. You can't make these decisions, however, unless you have a clear idea of where your money is going.

Also, under- and over-estimating how much you are spending on certain areas is very common. That's why you need to sit down and add it all up – this gives you a more realistic perspective. In more than 90 per cent of cases, people are surprised by the results. That proves that most of us really don't have a clue how much we are spending on certain things and categories.

Measuring your surplus cash flow

Your surplus cash flow is how much money you have left over after you pay for all expenses and outgoings. Your income is typically easy to measure or ascertain, you can simply look at your pay slips or tax return. However, expenses and outgoings can be a little more difficult to get a hold on.

Typically, I find the best way to measure your expenditure is to go over your last three months of transactions from your bank accounts and credit card statements and allocate your expenditure into seven categories.

The easiest way to do this is to download the last three months of transactions into a spreadsheet via internet banking (most banks provide this functionality). You can then sort the spreadsheet by 'description'. This will typically group similar expenses together. In a spare column, you then can enter the expense category you want the transaction to be allocated to. (I outline possible categories in the following list.) When you have allocated each expense to a category, sort the spreadsheet by category and add the total for each category. This high-level approach should be sufficient to give you a good handle on your expenditure levels and where your money is going.

The seven categories I recommend are:

1. Financial commitments – for example, rent, mortgages, car lease and child support.

2. Utilities – including costs for gas, electricity, rates, phone, water, internet and contents insurance.

3. Health and education – such as school fees, health insurance, medical expenses and child care.

4. Shopping and transport – for example, food, clothing, beauty, petrol, car maintenance and public transport expenses.

5. Entertainment – include here costs for holidays, gifts, eating out, movies and coffees.

6. Cash – include all withdrawals from ATMs. (If this figure is high, stop using ATMs and start using EFTPOS or credit cards more often because doing so makes tracking where you are spending your money much easier. Remember, you can't manage what you can't measure.)

7. Other – include here anything that doesn't fit in the preceding categories.

For further help with recording and organising your expenses, go to www.investopoly.com.au, where you can find a video that takes you through the process.

When you start to analyse your expenditure by category, no doubt you will come across non-reoccurring and/or extraordinary items. Non-reoccurring items are once-off expenses that are unlikely to reoccur in the future – such as major surgery or your child's wedding. An extraordinary item is one that is unusually high for that expense category, such as major motor vehicle repairs. It is necessary to adjust for non-reoccurring and extraordinary items by excluding them when determining your future maintainable surplus cash flow. However, if some 'lumpy' items do seem to reoccur spasmodically a few times over the year, you probably need to make an annual allowance for them. For example, if you have an old home or car that tends to require maintenance and you have had to pay for many 'once-off' breakdowns and repairs over the last few years, this is likely to be an ongoing expense.

Once you have completed this analysis you should be able to calculate what you spend each month on average. You can then work out what your annual surplus investable cash flow is – that is, income left over after paying for all expenses.

What about unforeseen expenses?

Life is full of surprises – including financial surprises – good and bad! A large bill could arise from time to time without warning or you may need to travel unexpectedly. You can accommodate or prepare for these nasty surprises in one of two ways:

1. When you allocate surplus cash flow towards an investment strategy, don't allocate all of it. For example, if a client has $2,000 of surplus cash flow per month, I would recommend that they don't embark on an investment that commits

(maybe due to borrowings) any more than, say, $1,200 per month. This leaves a buffer of $800 per month.

2. Ensure you hold cash savings equal to six months of living expenses. These cash savings can consist of savings in a bank account or extra repayments you have made into your home loan that can be redrawn if needed at any time.

The preceding two options should provide you with the necessary financial resources to weather most storms.

Perhaps a more detailed analysis might be required

Sometimes reviewing the past three months of expenses doesn't provide a reliable indication of your expenditure. This might be because the past three months have included a lot of changes or unusual expenses, or perhaps because you're surprised by the result. That is, if you review the last three months and the results show you are spending a lot more (or even a lot less) than you expected, you should review a longer period to ensure your findings are reliable. Simply select a longer period of time (say, the last 12 months) and allocate each expense. If using the spreadsheet method already described becomes a little tricky with the increased number of transactions, you can use some of the budgeting tools covered in the following section.

Budgeting tools

The Australian government's Australian Securities & Investments Commission (ASIC) operates a website called MoneySmart, which contains a number of useful calculators including a budget planner. Go to www.moneysmart.gov.au and, under the 'Calculators & resources' tab, select 'Budgeting, saving & tax calculators'. You will find the Budget Planner tool here, which allows you to track your historical expenditure using a web-based calculator or through downloading an Excel spreadsheet. The resources are very easy to use and allow you to quickly analyse the data you enter (to create an annual budget).

I have also developed an easy-to-use spreadsheet that you can access at no cost. To download this tool, simply go to www. investopoly.com.au.

In addition, your bank might provide tools that are integrated with its online banking. For example, ANZ offers a MoneyManager tool, NAB provides Money Tracker and CBA has My Spend. These tools automatically analyse your spending habits and provide a good indication of where your money is going.

How often do you need to do this?

Undertaking a high-level budget review at least every 12 to 18 months is a good idea – just to ensure that you are broadly on track. However, if you are trying to alter your spending habits (in other words, rein in spending), you need to review your spending every one to two months. This will allow you to make adjustments sooner – before things get too out of control.

If you have a partner, involving them in this process and getting their buy-in is very important. Let them know you're going to review expenditure and why it's important. Share the outcomes of your analysis (or get your partner involved in this analysis) and, if you feel it's important to reduce expenses, ask them where they think expenses can be pulled back. (The following section provides more help with identifying where these areas may be.)

Reviewing your expenses and budgeting with your partner is a good exercise to do in conjunction with developing a longer term financial plan. If your long-term goals are important to your partner, hopefully they will see that improving the management and tracking of your cash flow will help you both achieve these goals.

What to do if you don't have surplus income

As I discussed at the beginning of this chapter, cash flow management is the cornerstone of any wealth accumulation strategy. Without good cash flow discipline, any subsequent investment strategies or tactics will be doomed to failure. If your investigations suggest that you are spending all your income (or, worse still, more than your income), the following sections provide a few strategies you can consider implementing.

Don't reduce expenditure, reduce regularity

Find the discretionary items you spend the most amount of money on and, instead of cutting the amount you spend in one fell swoop, reduce the regularity of spending. Let me explain using an example. Say your partner and you love eating out at fine-dining restaurants and you have identified that you spend approximately $1,000 per month on such culinary adventures. That equates to $12,000 p.a. which (assuming interest rates are 7 per cent p.a.) is nearly enough to pay for an investment property's holding costs!

Of course, you could decide not to eat out anymore. However, my view is that if it's something you truly love doing and get a lot of enjoyment from, you should do it – life is too short. However, instead of spending $1,000 per month, maybe you could spend $500 every two months? In this way, you still get to enjoy the experience of a lovely meal with a nice bottle of wine, but your 'sacrifice' is that you do it less often. This approach is likely to be a lot easier to stick to and therefore be more successful. Life is about balancing your enjoyment of financial rewards now while still saving for the future.

Save what you don't have ... yet

Another way to add to your investable surplus income is to save future income. Many people receive regular pay reviews. What typically happens, however, is that people tend to adjust their spending habits in line with their income – if their income increases, so does their spending. Their overall 'standard of living' or 'pleasure', meanwhile, isn't impacted nearly as much – perhaps they simply buy a couple of coffees per day instead of one, and so on.

One way to prevent this slippage is to make a commitment to save a predetermined percentage of any future pay rises. For example, perhaps commit to 70 to 80 per cent of all future pay rises going towards investing, with the rest used for lifestyle items. This is often a painless way to help you accumulate a larger amount of investable surplus in the future.

Make windfall gains work hard for you

Sometimes we receive money unexpectedly – perhaps via a work bonus, inheritance or tax return refund. In such circumstances, spending these monies on frivolous items is very tempting – and you won't miss money that you never really had in the first place. However, making a commitment before you receive windfall gains can be an easy way to avoid this trap. Perhaps you can commit to investing a certain percentage of all future windfall gains. Again, it's unrealistic for most people to invest 100 per cent of these gains, but investing a certain percentage (maybe between 50 and 80 per cent) still gives you the room to enjoy life today while saving for the future at the same time.

Stop living beyond your means

Of course, a possible explanation for your woes is that you are living well beyond your means. In this case, you have to make some significant adjustments and they are likely to be painful. But since you are reading this book, you are likely ready and open to making such changes.

At the end of the day, if you are spending all your income and have little to no surplus, you must change your spending habits if you are to build wealth. This is not an easy process for many people. It takes discipline and maturity – but it can be done. You just need to find the approach that works for you.

Changing spending habits is like knocking over a fridge. You can't do it in one push. You have to rock it back and forth a few times, and then it goes over. In other words, change your spending habits gradually, bit by bit. After some time, you will start to see results and probably start enjoying the process. The following sections provide further help with changing spending habits.

The science of spending

The following list outlines 11 ideas I would like to share to help you better understand, manage and optimise your spending habits. These ideas have been gleaned from many behavioural theories[1] and my own personal and professional experiences. They are listed in no particular order.

Think about these ideas when looking to optimise your spending habits:

1. Professor Dan Ariely coined the term 'the pain of paying', which essentially states that paying for something using cash is a lot more painful than using card (or direct debit). Research has confirmed that people spend less (up to half!) if they use cash compared to a credit card. Delaying payment until after delivery of the goods (for example, using a

payment option such as Afterpay) ironically turns out to be the most painful payment method – don't use it! Therefore, maybe it's a good idea for you to use cash for all discretionary spending?

2. Experiences have a far greater impact on our happiness than things do. Research has shown that to maximise your happiness per dollar, you should spend money on experiences (such as holidays and doing things) rather than things (such as clothing and electronics). Therefore, if you need to reduce your spending, reduce spending on 'things' before you reduce spending on experiences.

3. Linking in with the preceding idea, money spent on creating more time for you to participate in enjoyable activities and pastimes will give you more enjoyment than simply buying more things. For example, spend less money on clothing and get a housekeeper – so you can spend more time with friends instead of cleaning.

4. Allocating yourself a weekly discretionary spending budget is a good idea and, when doing so, starting the weekly allocation on a Monday is best. Research has found that people who started their allocation on a Friday tended to spend their entire weekly budget over the weekend and, therefore, found it hard to stick to the budget during the working week.

5. Research also confirms that paying for a holiday a few months in advance significantly increases your enjoyment of that holiday. Firstly, once you have paid for it, you will naturally think about it more and, secondly, you have reduced the 'pain of paying' once you are on the holiday. One practical tip here: make sure you have travel insurance if you are going to prepay.

6. If you're spending too much on discretionary items, you'll probably find trimming 20 expenditure items by 5 per cent each a lot less painful than eliminating one item by 100 per cent. As already mentioned in this chapter, don't deny yourself in totality because it's painful! Much like a 'cheat day' for a diet, you must allow yourself to continue to enjoy the things you love. Just reduce the cost per item or experience, or do it less frequently.

7. You still need to reward yourself regularly. Research tells us that if you do, you will be a more successful saver and investor. The rewards don't have to be expensive (obviously), and can simply be something you love and enjoy and will look forward to. The more regular the rewards (say, monthly or quarterly), the more effectual they will be. Therefore, if you set yourself a spending/savings goal, attach a reward to it – for example, a massage or dinner out with your partner. Make sure the goal is attainable and realistic. Start small and then stretch the goal each consecutive period. Changing spending habits tends to take a bit of time – few people can go cold turkey.

8. Try delaying discretionary spending by two weeks. You know how it goes: you are out shopping, see something that takes your fancy, you buy it, take it home and it's never seen again (that is, it sits in the cupboard and is never used). Wastage! Spending $20, $50 or $80 on some items for the house or on clothes you will never wear really does add up. It is relatively easy to waste $5,000 to $10,000 per year on such items. You can avoid this by committing to a 'two-week rule'. If you see something you like, write it down. If in two weeks you still want to buy the item, buy it (using cash not card). This rule will help curtail impulsive spending and is less painful

because you are not saying 'no', just 'not yet'. We can live without most of the 'stuff' we have so you'll likely find this little rule quite helpful.

9. Consider whether you only need to budget for or keep track of a handful of items. Personally, 95 per cent of my discretionary spending goes on two items – eating out and wine. Therefore, for me to rein in my spending, I only have to track or budget for these two items. Budgeting doesn't have to be an overwhelming project that absorbs a lot of time and energy.

10. Research suggests that humans get more excited about the future than the past. Therefore, plan your purchases. If your goal is to buy a new handbag or special bottle of wine this year, plan it – set a future date when you will buy it. Research your purchase. You'll spend more time thinking about the item and so maximise your 'enjoyment per dollar'.

11. Finally, research shows spending money on other people (loved ones or charity) gives you the most amount of enjoyment. Again, as Tony Robbins says, 'living is about giving'.

Some tips to improve your cash flow management

Once you've starting changing your thinking about spending, you can do a few simple things to make saving money a lot easier. Here are a few ideas:

- **Pay yourself first:** In Stephen R. Covey's best-selling book, *The 7 Habits of Highly Effective People*, he suggests that you should always do the most important task first. Saving for your future is both important and urgent. Therefore, as soon as you get paid you should carve off a certain amount of income towards investing and saving. Do this before you do anything else.

- **Separate savings from transactional monies:** The saying 'out of sight, out of mind' is very helpful when it comes to saving. Use multiple savings or loan offset accounts to funnel your income into and delink these accounts from your internet banking profile – so you can't see the balances. Only retain a minimum balance in any transactional accounts so you're not ever tempted to spend the funds available. Putting a few road blocks in place will force you to think twice (or thrice) before you withdraw and spend your savings.

- **Take advantage of direct salary credit:** Many employers will allow you to nominate multiple accounts for pay deposits, meaning you can direct cash either into savings accounts or directly into your home loan to reduce debt. This might help you improve your cash flow management. Again, if you can't see it, you can't spend it!

Be realistic: Recognise your weaknesses

If you know you're not good at managing money, act accordingly. Put in place some of the ideas I have discussed in this chapter that automate saving and/or take it out of your hands. Also, think about whether you are better off not having a credit card (or one with a very low limit). Do not buy anything unless you can pay cash (so no store credit either). Get back to basics. Take control and write down some rules that you can follow. The financial services industry is designed to sell you more and more credit. That is their business. They are like drug dealers. So just beware!

If you're still having problems, get help from a good accountant

If you're still having trouble managing your cash flow after trying the tips outlined in this chapter, it might be time to call the accountants in! A good accountant will be able to use technology (such as cloud accounting) to help you manage your cash flow more effectively. This involves using software to automatically categorise your spending (using transactional information feeds provided by your bank) and producing monthly reports. As I have said throughout this chapter, you can't manage what you don't measure. The accountant can also ensure your bank accounts are structured in a way that facilitates better management. The demand for this type of service has increased dramatically over the past few years in our practice. You need to learn how to manage cash flow – people aren't born with these skills.

Golden Rule #3 summary

To master your cash flow, you need to understand the following:

- Most of good cash flow management is knowing where your money goes. If you track your expenditure every 6 to 12 months, you'll likely find that you naturally adjust your spending habits. The number one failure most people make is not tracking.

- Budgeting is not a dirty word. It doesn't mean saving as much as possible and not enjoying any pleasurable experiences. The role of budgeting is to get the most amount of pleasure per dollar. If it's not adding to the enjoyment of life, cut it.

- To measure your cash flow, simply review the past three months of outgoings and allocate expenditure into seven core categories.

- The goal of managing cash flow is to quantify your investable surplus income – that is, the amount of income that you can allocate towards an investment strategy. Most investment strategies will require a commitment of a regular contribution over many years.

- Many tips and strategies for reducing expenditure and/or increasing your surplus investable income are available. Much like dieting, you just need to find what works for you. Life is a balance, and you need to balance enjoying some pleasure today with investing for tomorrow.

- If you're still struggling with cash flow management, seek help from an accountant. They can automate much of the process and produce month reports. They will also be able to help you structure your bank accounts effectively.

Once you have mastered cash flow, move on...

Mastering your cash flow is important. You must commit to contributing a certain amount of surplus cash flow towards your retirement strategy each and every year. Once you have done that, you are ready to move forward with your investment journey.

---

1   Some of the ideas included in this list are gleaned from *Happy Money: The New Science of Smarter Spending* by Elizabeth Cullen Dunn and Michael Norton and published by Simon & Schuster, and from *Dollars and Sense: Money Mishaps and How to Avoid Them* by Dan Ariely and Jeff Kreisler and published by Pan Macmillan.

GROW YOUR ASSET BASE AND THEN TILT TOWARDS INCOME

Everyone knows that you need to build a house in a certain order. First you lay the foundations to provide enough strength to support the walls. Once the walls are erected, you can then put the roof on. You can't build a house in an ad hoc manner – for example, build a little bit of the foundations, then some of the roof, then some walls and then back to the foundations. There's a right and wrong way to build a house. The same is true for investing. You must invest in asset classes in the right order to efficiently build wealth.

This chapter sets out the order in which you should invest and why. It also shows you how to develop an investment strategy and what you must consider – including a walk-through of a typical investment strategy life cycle.

Why investing for income is wrong

Strategy without tactics is the slowest route to victory.
Tactics without strategy is the noise before defeat.

Commonly attributed to Sun Tzu, author of *The Art of War*

A common error that new investors make when developing an investment strategy is thinking they should invest for income from the beginning. The theory goes that someday they would like to cease employment (and, therefore, they need to replace personal exertion income), so they should invest in assets that generate a passive income stream. While this is true, it is not the most efficient strategy.

The main problem with investing for income is you lose too much of your investment return through the payment of income tax. While you're working, you're already paying a lot of income tax. Your investments generating a large amount of passive income will only add to your tax bill. As such, you might end up sending around 40 per cent of your investment return back to the government in taxes. Because of this, you will have less money (after tax) to reinvest.

Why income alone won't work

Let's compare income assets to assets that generate an overall return of 10 per cent p.a. each. The only difference between the two investments is the components of the return – one asset produces more income (and, therefore, less growth) than the other. As you can see from the following table, the investment that generates less income results in a lower tax expense and, therefore, a 1 per cent p.a. higher after-tax return. However, most importantly, the higher capital growth rate for asset two makes a massive difference on the value of the asset over the long run. Asset one is projected to be worth $1.45 million in 20 years, whereas asset two is projected to be worth $2.33 million – some $880,000 more. The point is, all things being equal, it's very valuable to substitute less income in return for more capital growth.

	Asset one	Asset two
Income	4.5%	2.0%
Capital growth	5.5%	8.0%
Tax on income @ 40%	(1.8%)	(0.8%)
After-tax total return	8.2%	9.2%
Value of asset in 20 years	@ 5.5% p.a. growth: $1.45m	@ 8% p.a. growth: $2.33m

Note that the preceding table only includes the impact of income tax. It does not include the impact of capital gains tax, which, of course, all investors will pay on any capital gains they make when they sell the investment.

The following table sets out the after-tax returns produced by each asset after paying for income and capital gains tax. The amounts shown represent the after-tax income plus capital returns. It is important to note that asset two produces a 21 per cent higher return (at $400,000 more).

	Asset one	Asset two
Total after-tax returns after 20 years (minus income tax + capital gains tax)	$1.88m	$2.28m

You need to build wealth in two steps

In a way, building wealth is very similar to playing golf. When you play golf, the goal is to hit the ball into the hole using the least number of shots (that is, with the greatest efficiency). For example, you wouldn't tee off using a putter because a putter is designed for accuracy, not distance. It's not the right club for the shot.

Investing is no different. A good investment strategy will consist of investing in the right assets, in the right *order*, to build wealth in the most efficient way. Typically, the most efficient way to become independently wealthy is to first build your asset base. Once you have a strong asset base, you then use that asset base to start investing for income.

For example, consider the situation where someone wants to retire, expects to live for another 30 to 40 years and has a net asset base of $500,000. If they approached me and asked me to develop an investment strategy for them, it would be obvious to me that they didn't have a sufficient asset base to achieve the goal. However, if their net worth was, say, $5 million, we could draw upon many strategies to help them fund retirement. The crudest strategy (just to illustrate this point) would be potentially to sell all the assets and put the money in the bank and live off the interest. After paying for capital gains tax, I estimate that their cash savings would generate well over $100,000 in year in interest. I'm not suggesting that I would recommend this strategy but merely making the point that if you build your asset base, you will have plenty of options to fund retirement. Therefore, my advice to you is to focus all your efforts on building your asset base (meaning focus on capital growth), with less focus on passive income.

Understanding the power of compounding capital growth

Compound interest is the eighth wonder of the world.
He who understands it, earns it ... he who doesn't, pays it.

Commonly misattributed to Albert Einstein

If you are to only learn and remember one concept from reading this book I would very much like it to be this one. The power of compounding capital growth is the fundamental financial concept that can help people realise the benefit of investing in quality assets and holding those assets for a long period of time. This one strategy does most of the heavy lifting in terms of building your net worth.

Simply put, compounding capital growth is like rolling a snowball downhill. The longer the hill, the more momentum the snowball builds and the larger it will become. The same is true with investment assets. The longer we hold investment-grade assets, the more substantial the impact compounding capital growth has on our asset base. The following chart goes some way to illustrate this.

$500k asset grows by 8% p.a. over 30 years

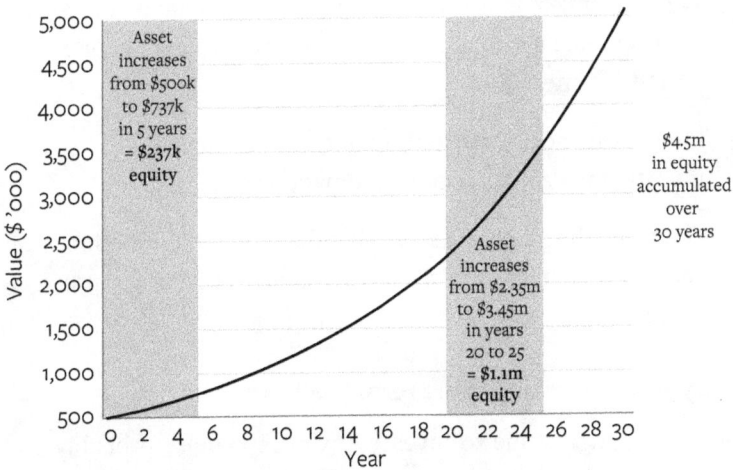

Asset increases from $500k to $737k in 5 years = $237k equity

$4.5m in equity accumulated over 30 years

Asset increases from $2.35m to $3.45m in years 20 to 25 = $1.1m equity

Value ($'000)

Year

The preceding chart graphs the value of an asset purchased for $500,000 over 30 years, assuming its growth rate is 8 per cent per annum. Please note that 8 per cent is the average annual growth rate over a 30-year period. An investment asset is highly unlikely to produce a uniform growth rate each year – instead, growth is invariably volatile. However, for the sake of this illustration, I have averaged out the growth rate over the 30 years.

The chart is separated into five-year periods. You will note that the growth in the first five years is approximately $237,000. Compare that with the growth between years 20 and 25 – in this five-year period, the dollar value growth is $1.1 million. Therefore, in the later five-year period the investor is enjoying over four times more growth in dollar value – an average of over $200,000 per year.

You can also take some other key learnings away from this chart:

- The sooner we start investing, the sooner our assets will start producing significant growth in dollar value terms

- We must invest in assets that possess the fundamentals that help generate a strong level of capital growth over a long period of time

- One of the most important ingredients in an astute investment strategy is time and patience

- Compounding capital growth is substantially more important than income when it comes to investment assets (as already discussed).

Are you still thinking short term?

Is now the right time to invest? Anxious? You are probably still thinking too short term!

One of the most common causes for investor procrastination is the anxiety created by worrying about short-term market movements. That is, many investors (particularly inexperienced investors) agonise over whether now is the right time to start investing. They wonder whether, alternatively, they should wait another three to six months just to see if the market moves. This idea is premised on the assumption that in three to six months' time, things will be a little clearer and they will feel more confident to invest. What they don't realise is that in three to six months' time a whole new set of circumstances will likely produce uncertainty. If you are waiting for a 'utopian' time – when you feel 100 per cent confident with your proposed investments – it will probably never arrive. Uncertainty will always be present – you are just going to have to learn to live with it.

The best way to deal with this anxiety is to approach investing with a long-term view. Remind yourself that you're investing today for the long term. As such, the performance of investments in the short to medium term is largely inconsequential. For example, if you purchase an investment property today for $500,000 and you plan to retire in 20 years' time, your only concern should be ascertaining the likelihood of said property being worth in the order of $1.5 to $2 million by the time you get to retirement. What the property is worth in 24 months' time is not important.

Taking a long-term approach forces you to focus on the things that really matter and not get distracted by shiny objects or short-term noise. Long-term investors are forced to focus on the underlying fundamentals of an investment, because the fundamentals will drive the investment performance long after any market noise or hysteria dissipates.

This is why experienced investors tend to become more successful over time. They learn through their own experiences that, in the fullness of time, the fundamentals (quality) of any investment dictate its performance. Therefore, they know that buying a quality asset in any market and holding that asset for a long period of time will likely generate substantial wealth. Because they have experienced this in the past and so have more confidence, these investors find having the discipline of ignoring any media hype, hysteria, noise and so on a lot easier.

> *Life isn't about waiting for the storm to pass ...*
> *It's about learning to dance in the rain.*
>
> Vivian Greene

Superannuation and other investments and timing

Most Australians have superannuation savings. The main question you need to ask is how long your superannuation will last in retirement. If you're projected to have significant superannuation savings by the time you reach retirement, you probably don't have to worry too much about investing in other assets. However, if you're like most Australians, either you won't have enough super to fund your retirement or the amount of super you have won't fund the standard of retirement you desire.

You could argue that any investing you do in addition to your super will play one of two roles:

1. It will supplement your superannuation savings – that is, the existence of other investments will mean that you won't need to draw as much money from super.

2. It will assist you in funding retirement after you have used your super. In this situation, super might fund the first 'phase' of retirement (for example, maybe the first 10 years) and then your other assets will fund the second phase of retirement (such as after the first 10 years of retirement).

Once again, this means you're able to take a very long-term view with such investments, because you don't need these investments to produce passive income for a considerable amount of time.

This is even more reason not to worry or be influenced by short-term market changes and volatility.

How capital growth will help fund retirement

A common question I receive relates to how investing in property (for example) can help fund retirement. This question is driven by the understanding that property (especially houses compared to apartments) generates a relatively small amount of income compared to its value (which is referred to as yield).

Therefore, many people correctly calculate that they would need to own a significant amount of property in dollar terms (net of any loans) to generate income sufficient to fund living expenses. For example, if we assume we are able receive a net (after expenses) rental yield of, say, 2 per cent p.a. from property and you need an annual income of, say, $100,000 to fund retirement, you need to own unencumbered property worth $5 million to generate said income. This is one solution.

However, unless you start investing in your twenties and/or have a considerable amount of income, it's unlikely you will be able to amass that much equity. That, however, doesn't mean investing in property is not the right approach. You can employ a few other strategies to help you fund retirement:

- *Sell down your assets in an orderly fashion:* One strategy that you can consider utilising is the possible sale of an investment property. Of course, the major downside of selling an asset is that it costs money to do so, with the two major costs being agent fees (and related marketing expenses) and capital gains tax. You might be able to minimise the amount of capital gains tax you pay, depending on the property's ownership structure. If you think your investment strategy might include the sale of assets, this is something you need to consider in your ownership plan. Selling an asset will obviously generate a large cash holding. You can either use these cash savings to fund living expenses in retirement and/ or direct them towards debt repayment.

- *Focus on small yield, high-value property*: As discussed earlier in this chapter, it is possible to amass significant equity in property if you hold it for long enough. This may be the case if you started your investment journey in your twenties or early thirties. However, it might be possible to hold onto your investment properties longer if you fund the initial part of your retirement entirely from super.

- *Use equity to invest for income*: Once you have accumulated a reasonably strong asset base using property and/or shares, it might be appropriate for you to borrow against that equity to invest in income-style assets. For example, an astute strategy might include investing in residential property initially (to build a strong asset base), and then borrowing against the equity to invest in commercial property primarily for income. Taking this approach allows you to tilt your asset base towards more income-style assets. In the fullness of time, this should give you a nice balance of both capital growth and income.

- *Sell and redistribute the wealth into income-style assets*: An adaption of the first strategy in this list includes selling an asset and investing the net cash proceeds into income-style assets. For example, if you had, say, three investment properties, you might decide to sell one and retain two. You could use those net cash proceeds from the sale of the investment property and invest those monies in a high-yielding share fund and/or a (investment-grade corporate and mortgage-backed) bond portfolio.

Focus on developing a strategy

I've already discussed in Golden Rule #2 how not starting with a clear idea of your investment goals is like jumping in your car with no idea of where you're headed, and so driving around aimlessly. Investing without goals means you end up making ad-hoc investment decisions with little comfort that what you are doing is enough (and not too much) to achieve your goals.

The same applies to developing your investment strategy. Without a strategy, you won't know if you're taking the most efficient path. On the other hand, developing an investment strategy allows you to compare various options and select the one that exhibits the lowest risk and the highest probability of working. Undertaking this analysis before you invest can save wasting a lot of time heading down the wrong path. Should you invest in property? Invest in the share market? Make additional contributions into super? These are all valid options and you can't select the best one until you develop an investment strategy (which you will be able to do after reading this book).

An investment strategy doesn't have to be a massively comprehensive and tedious project. In fact, it is my view that often the simplest plans work best. The point is you need to have a clear idea about what you need to do over the next 10, 20 and perhaps 30 years to achieve your financial goals. Your strategy might be as simple as investing in two properties and making additional contributions into super. If you work out that that level of investing will be sufficient to fund retirement, you don't need to worry any further. That said, many investors don't even get that far.

How do you develop a strategy?

Developing a reliably sound investment strategy requires two ingredients.

Firstly, you need knowledge and experience. Knowledge can be gained from books such as this one. Experience can be gained through speaking with other investors so that you can vicariously benefit from their learnings, mistakes and successes. I cannot stress how important 'experience' is. As they say, 'Most people learn through making mistakes, smart people learn from other people's mistakes and dumb people never learn!' Of course, another solution involves seeking professional advice from an independent financial planner (read the final chapter in this book before deciding whether to do this or not).

Secondly, you need to develop a financial model that includes projections for your income, expenses, assets and liabilities. When I develop strategies for clients, I typically use a projection period of 30 years. Of course, all financial projections have an inherent level of uncertainty – and the longer dated the projections, the higher the level of uncertainty. Just because financial projections possess a level of uncertainty, however, doesn't mean they are worthless. In fact, it is critically important that we make some attempt to work out the possible financial outcomes from implementing a certain investment strategy. Without this analysis, we would be flying blind.

The purpose of the financial model is to ensure that your chosen strategy will achieve your financial goals, namely:

- providing enough passive income to fund your living expenses in retirement

- creating enough wealth so that you don't run out of money in retirement.

You use your financial model to help you develop an investment strategy. Essentially, you financially compare various tactics – such as buying an investment property versus making additional super contributions versus investing in shares versus repaying debt (home loan) and so on – or a combination of these tactics. Typically, after modelling various scenarios, one or two strategies stand out as superior ones.

The financial model must be comprehensive enough to deal with all taxes, investment characteristics, ownership structures, cash flow outcomes and so on. Even a small omission or error could materially affect the reliability of the financial model. To be honest, these complex requirements mean most people don't have the required knowledge and skill to prepare their own financial projections. Therefore, my advice is to seek professional help. You may need to find an experienced accountant or financial planner who can help you financially model your investment strategy to ensure it will help you achieve your goals.

It is also important that any financial model adopts conservative and considered assumptions. When determining the assumptions you will use, you really should do a lot of homework. They need to be as accurate as possible. If the assumptions are incorrect, then the model has a higher probability of being incorrect.

An hour invested on strategy could save you years

How much time you spend developing your strategy is just like almost everything else in life – that is, it's about balance. Spending no time developing a strategy is foolhardy and destined for failure. But getting too bogged down in developing a strategy is a mistake too – it is possible to over-analyse! You need to find a balance. Your only goal is to have a clear idea of what you need to do over the next 5, 10, 15 and 20 years to achieve your goals. You don't necessarily need a 40-page financial plan – often a plan summarised on one page can be just as useful.

Again (I can't stress this enough!) spending a bit of time mapping out what you need to do and what types of assets will underpin your plan now could save you wasting years heading down the wrong path.

If you are going to spend any money on getting advice, strategy development is the place to spend it. If you do seek professional advice, please make sure that you read the final chapter in this book before doing so.

Ownership structures are part of strategy

How will you own your investment? In your personal name? In a family trust? In superannuation? The structuring of investments is an important consideration when developing an investment strategy. The following table outlines my thoughts on the most common structures. (All aspects quoted, including applicable tax rates, are correct at the time of writing. These may change in the future, which may affect the appropriateness of the ownership structure. Therefore, you should seek personal advice from a registered tax agent prior to investing.)

While I am a registered tax agent, you should of course obtain personalised tax advice from a licensed professional to ensure that your plans are appropriate. The table opposite is a summary only and is intended to just give you an idea of what structures to use and when.

As with most things in life, diversification is the key here. Each ownership structure has its pros and cons and no one structure is 'perfect'. However, you can achieve perfection, to some degree, at a portfolio level, by spreading your assets across various ownership structures.

Structure	Pros	Cons	General comment
Personal name	If you are borrowing to invest in an asset, you can claim the interest as a tax deduction, thereby reducing your overall tax (negative gearing)	No flexibility to tax-effectively stream income or capital gains to save tax now and in retirement	Most people will benefit from holding some assets in their personal name; if you have a spouse, try to spread your wealth between you
Family trust	Ability to allocate income and capital gains to different people each year to minimise tax; provides some estate planning and asset protection benefits	Any tax losses are trapped inside the trust and carried forward (i.e. no immediate negative gearing benefits)	Typically, family trusts better suit self-employed/business owners (not employees) and/or people who plan on holding large share market investments
Company	Flat tax rate of 27.5% applied for small business entities	A company is not entitled to the 50% capital gains tax discount, and little flexibility exists in how income and capital is distributed	A company is appropriate in very limited circumstances
Superannuation	Tax rate of 15% applies on income and 10% on capital gains; nil tax in retirement on balances less than $1.6m	Your money is locked away until age 60 (or possibly later if the government changes the rules in the future)	The tax benefits of super are too attractive to be ignored, meaning most people will be well served by accumulating some wealth inside super

For example, for employees, investing in property in personal names and then investing in shares, bonds and cash inside super – and possibly a family trust (for people with substantial wealth) – is typically best. For self-employed business owners, investing in property in a family trust and in shares, bonds and cash in super might be best.

Another aspect to consider is that certain types of investments suit certain ownership structures. For example, an investment that is expected to provide a high level of income (such as a commercial property) might be best suited to ownership within a self-managed super fund (because, at the time of writing, income is taxed at 15 per cent). Of course, this is a generalisation – but I wanted to give you a feeling for how different assets suit different structures.

You must consider various other implications in additional to income tax. For example, property land tax is an insidious tax – that is, it tends to sneak up on you after many years of ownership and is most severe in retirement – so it's worthy of consideration. In many states, family trusts pay a higher rate of land tax than individuals and SMSFs. Therefore, if you plan to hold multiple investment properties, holding them across multiple ownership structures (for example, one in each person's name and one in an SMSF) will help you minimise your land tax expense.

Other things you also need to consider include any cash flow implications, estate planning (for example, your ability to transfer wealth to your spouse and/or children), asset protection and the ability to fund your investment plans (that is, your ability to borrow). This aspect of funding your investment plans is the topic of this next section.

Financing your strategy

A strategy, even a great one, doesn't implement itself.

Jeroen De Flander

Developing an investment strategy is one thing; being able to implement it is another. Most investment strategies will require some amount of borrowings – in fact, including some borrowings is often essential to making your income and equity work hard for you. The key is to get the balance right. You don't want to over-borrow and risk losing money and causing a lot of financial stress – or, worse still, pushing retirement further away because you have to keep working to service loans. But not borrowing is not the answer either!

You can use your cash flow in two ways. Firstly, of course, you can use borrowings to allow you to invest more money upfront. For example, borrowing and investing $500,000 today in one hit is far better than investing $2920[1] per month over the next 30 years (assuming a 10 per cent p.a. investment return) – which is your second option. The difference in today's dollars in 30 years' time is over $1.3 million (or 43 per cent more wealth)!

As well as providing increased returns, borrowing also allows you to reduce your risk – because it allows you to build in buffers (that is, access to money in the case of unforeseen expenses or events). Also, to some extent, it negates one of the downsides to holding property – its illiquidity.

To be a successful investor you must maximise and proactively manage your borrowing capacity. To do this you need to enlist the assistance of an experienced mortgage broker and educate yourself about the 'game' of borrowing. Excuse the shameless plug but, if you need further information on this topic, I have written a book that focuses on it – *Smart Borrowers Handbook*, plus an endless supply of great articles and advice is available online.

In short, do not overlook the importance of proactively managing your borrowing capacity.

Periodic reviews: compare to projections

Having a strategy gives you a *context* for making future financial decisions. For example, if your plan includes purchasing an investment property in the next 12 months, you might decide to postpone renovations to your home so that you are able to execute on your investment – because you know that postponing the investment will compromise your ability to reach your financial goals. Or, maybe you are in a far better financial position than you expected to be when you developed your plan five years ago, so taking the family on an overseas holiday is something that is now easily affordable. Having a clear context is very important and helps avoid making decisions you may regret in the future.

Most decisions have short-, medium- and longer-term consequences. Making the *right* decision is a matter of clearly understanding the consequences. Given the complete and correct information, most people make the right decision. *Wrong* decisions are typically made because people don't have a full appreciation of the short-, medium- and longer-term consequences.

This means reviewing your financial results periodically is important – and annually is often best. The goal of this exercise is to see if you are on track. If not, you can then take corrective action before it becomes a major problem.

The key items to consider are:

- *Are you allocating the right amount of cash flow towards your strategy?* If not, typically the main culprit is over-spending on living expenses. In this case, you may need to pull your spending back a bit.

- *Are your investments performing as expected?* That is, are you happy with your investment returns? Compare results to your initial projections to check whether they are on track – or whether you need to adjust your assets to meet your projections. You need to be very careful with this analysis, especially if you haven't held your investments for a reasonable period of time. Very few investments perform in a straight-line basis. Instead, returns are random and volatile, so you need to hold most investments for a long period of time (at least 10 or more years) to even out the randomness of returns (volatility). For example, with respect to residential investment property, in any ten-year period you might experience one to three years of excellent capital growth, maybe one year of negative growth and the rest of the time very little change in value. This is why it's possible to purchase an investment-grade asset and not see much capital growth in the first five years. This performance doesn't necessarily make it a poor asset, but does illustrate why getting independent, professional advice when selecting assets is so important.

- *Has your financial situation changed and, if so, does the strategy need to change too?* Consider things like changes in income, goals and circumstances.

A typical investment strategy life cycle

Just as you move through different stages in your life, so too does your investment strategy. The following outlines what to do at various stages of life:

- *In your twenties and early thirties:* Buy property first – the first thing a young person in their twenties or thirties should do is buy an investment-grade property, for two reasons. Firstly, it allows you to invest sooner – that is, you can access higher leverage because you can typically borrow 90 to 95 per cent of a property's value. Secondly, an investment-grade property provides most of its return in compounding capital growth.

- *In your thirties and forties:* Upgrade your home and buy investment property/s – the priority in this phase is asset acquisition. Although you will naturally have some lifestyle goals, such as upgrading your home to better accommodate your family, the main goal in this phase is to accumulate sufficient assets that will provide a robust amount of capital growth over the next 30 to 40 years.

- *In your late forties and fifties:* Repay/offset debt, contribute into super and invest in other assets such as shares – during this phase you should focus more on reducing liabilities and boosting your super balance. As you approach retirement, you should have a greater focus on generating more passive income (rather than capital growth).

- *From 60:* Draw an income stream from super – hopefully you should have sufficient super to fund the first portion of retirement (at least the first 10 years). You can do this by drawing a regular income from your super account. It is likely that this income will be tax-free.

- *10 to 20 years post retirement:* Divest of property assets – when your super balance is getting low, you should consider selling an investment property (if necessary). Since you (hopefully) purchased the property three to four decades ago, it should have generated substantial capital growth (if you invested in the right asset).

To clarify these ideas further, the following figure provides a graphical representation of this typical investment strategy life cycle. I discuss asset allocation in much further detail in the next chapter.

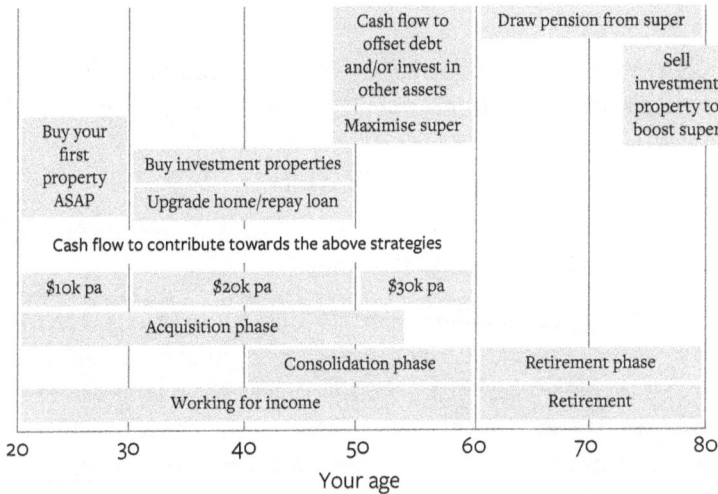

			Cash flow to offset debt and/or invest in other assets	Draw pension from super	
					Sell investment property to boost super
Buy your first property ASAP			Maximise super		
	Buy investment properties				
	Upgrade home/repay loan				
Cash flow to contribute towards the above strategies					
$10k pa	$20k pa		$30k pa		
Acquisition phase					
		Consolidation phase		Retirement phase	
Working for income				Retirement	

Your age: 20   30   40   50   60   70   80

- Compound capital growth will do all the heavy lifting in terms of building your wealth. To achieve this, you need to invest in quality assets that have the fundamentals to deliver strong growth over long periods of time, and have the time and patience to hold onto said assets.

- Short-term financial decisions might generate quick profit but rarely produce long-term value. Therefore, when making financial decisions, ask yourself what course of action will ensure you are financially stronger in 10, 20 and 30 years.

- Capital growth assets (such as property) can still help you fund retirement despite their low income.

- It is important to develop an investment strategy (even a basic one) for two reasons: firstly, to work out how much you need to invest to achieve your goals – you don't want to under-invest or over-invest – and, secondly, to ensure you have chosen the most efficient strategy that has the highest probability of working.

- The best way to formulate a strategy is to financially model the outcomes using a spreadsheet.

- Your investment strategy must consider ownership structures and your ability to fund your plan (borrowings).

- It is important to review your progress annually and compare your actual position to where you projected it to be. This will allow you to take any corrective action as soon as possible.

---

1 $2920 per month is the monthly interest cost on a $500,000 loan at an interest rate of 7 per cent p.a. The investor has the choice of, first, borrowing the lump sum, investing and using their cash flow to meet the interest expense. Alternatively, if they do not borrow, they could invest the equivalent amount each month. Mathematically, borrowing wins if the investment rents are higher than the interest rate.

GOLDEN RULE #5

SET YOUR ASSET ALLOCATION TO REDUCE RISK AND MAXIMISE RETURNS

American investor, economist and professor Benjamin Graham taught Warren Buffett investing has only two rules:

1. Never lose money

2. Refer to rule number one.

But how does this help you with what you should invest in? Should you focus on property, shares, bonds, commercial property, cash or something completely different? This question is called 'asset allocation' – that is, how you allocate your investment dollars towards different asset classes. In the previous chapter, I provided a basic timeline for asset allocation based on age and retirement.

This chapter lays out in more detail a methodical approach you can use to help you select the most appropriate asset allocation for you and your goals.

Before you get stuck into your investment strategy, you need to understand a few fundamental observations about asset allocation. Through this chapter, I have used historic data (returns and volatilities) to demonstrate why this is so important. In the absence of such understanding, you're highly likely to make costly mistakes. At the end of this chapter, I then share with you some example asset allocations you can adopt for your own strategy.

What is asset allocation?

Asset allocation involves the decision of how you will allocate your investment dollars towards various asset classes – such as shares, property, cash or bonds. Do you put all your money into direct residential property or everything in the share market? Or do you spread it across all major asset classes – and, if so, in what proportions? What is the right asset allocation?

Why is asset allocation an investor's most important decision?

Many academics and professionals regard asset allocation as an investor's most important decision – because your asset allocation determines your portfolio's performance, risk and volatility. By investing in different asset classes in different proportions, you should be able to minimise your probability of making a loss in any one year and, ultimately, maximise your long-term return.

To understand why asset allocation is so important we have to make friends with one very important fact (and one I have already highlighted in this book) – that is, that no-one knows which asset class will perform the best in the short term (say, over the next one to five years). No-one in the world has developed a reliable way of consistently predicting short-term asset class returns. If someone tells you that they know which direction an asset class (like shares or property) will move in the short term, walk – no, run – in the opposite direction. No-one has a crystal ball! We cannot control *markets* and, therefore, we cannot control *returns*. No-one can. Returns are random – which I will discuss in more detail later in this chapter.

Therefore, knowing this, we must invest in a way that, regardless of what happens (for example, shares are up while property is down, or bonds are up while shares are down), we have the best possible chance of generating a positive overall return – that is, not lose money. Put simply, you really need a finger in every pie.

Types of asset allocation methodologies

The two dominant types of asset allocation methodologies are strategic and tactical.

A *strategic* asset allocation is set based on an investor's risk profile and investment time horizon (how long until retirement), while also having consideration of long-term historical investment returns and volatility. For example, an investor who is very risk averse might allocate more of their monies to defensive assets like bonds and cash. Typically, you would rebalance a strategic asset allocation annually – I discuss what rebalancing is and why it's important in Golden Rule #6.

A *tactical* asset allocation is set based on the investor taking small, short-term views (bets) on asset classes and investing accordingly. For example, an investor might hold the view that the residential property market is overinflated and will crash. As such, they might invest their entire wealth in shares and bonds.

I believe that adopting a strategic asset allocation and making small tactical tilts is the best approach. This means that you decide the *range* you would like to invest in any one asset class – which then provides some flexibility to make tactical tilts depending on your views. For example, you might decide to invest 20 to 25 per cent of your total wealth in the Australian share market. If you are bearish (negative) about the Aussie stock market, maybe you reduce your exposure to, say, 20 per cent. But you certainly would not reduce the exposure to nil – on the basis that no-one knows what will happen, so we don't want to make massive bets. Instead, we still want to keep a finger in each pie.

Asset allocation and the impact of investing in residential property

Achieving a perfect asset allocation when investing in residential property is very difficult because it is such a lumpy asset – it's not like you can invest in one property in $10,000 increments. Therefore, my suggestion is to adopt two asset allocations:

1. One allocation should exclude direct property. This asset allocation will include all other major asset classes, such as shares, bonds and cash. As these asset classes are more liquid than property, you should be able to achieve a strategic weighting throughout your investment journey. You should consider your allocation at a total personal wealth perspective – for example, with respect to your share allocation, you should include shares held inside and outside of super.

2. The second allocation is the target asset allocation you would like to achieve by the time you reach retirement. This asset allocation will include all asset classes (that is, direct property as well). For example, direct property might be 90 per cent of your wealth today but, as your superannuation grows and you invest in other assets, direct property might represent,

say, 30 per cent of your total wealth by the time you reach retirement. In Golden Rule #4, I discussed the importance of investing in property sooner (to gain enough strong compounding growth) despite its negative impact on your asset allocation (that is, being heavily invested in property).

Achieving a perfectly balanced asset allocation each year throughout your investment journey is impossible if you invest in property. At the beginning, you will be very heavily invested in property. But, as time passes, you can balance this out. You can't do anything about this – and, so long as you are investing in quality assets, it should work out fine.

Can you spot a trend? Returns are random

The following table sets out the annual returns of various asset classes for each calendar year over a 24-year period (from 1996 through to 2016). Do you notice any trends in the returns? Are there any patterns? Nope! By the way, you can access a copy of this table on my website, where you can enlarge it to see more detail – go to www.investopoly.com.au.

Burton Malkiel popularised the theory that investment returns are entirely random and, therefore, cannot be predicted in his bestselling book from 1973, *A Random Walk Down Wall Street*. Malkiel argued that asset prices typically exhibit signs of a random 'walk' and that one cannot consistently outperform market averages. Website www.investopedia.com offers this follow-up to the story:

> In 1988, the *Wall Street Journal* created a contest to test Malkiel's random walk theory by creating the annual *Wall Street Journal* Dartboard Contest, pitting professional investors against darts for stock-picking supremacy. *Wall Street Journal* staff members played the role of the dart-throwing

Asset class returns from January 1996 to December 2016

Year	Australian shares (all ords)	International shares	US shares (S&P 500)	Cash	Australian bonds	International bonds (hedged)	Residential property
1996	14.6%	6.2%	15.0%	7.6%	11.9%	10.3%	9.8%
1997	12.2%	41.6%	62.7%	5.6%	12.2%	10.4%	11.7%
1998	11.6%	32.3%	36.7%	5.1%	9.5%	10.7%	8.4%
1999	16.1%	17.2%	13.7%	5.0%	-1.2%	0.4%	19.5%
2000	3.6%	2.2%	7.3%	6.3%	12.1%	9.8%	9.1%
2001	10.1%	-10.0%	-4.4%	5.2%	5.5%	7.2%	15.2%
2002	-8.5%	-27.4%	-29.8%	4.8%	8.8%	11.1%	12.9%
2003	16.4%	-0.8%	-2.9%	4.9%	3.0%	5.5%	12.2%
2004	27.7%	9.9%	6.8%	5.6%	7.0%	8.9%	-0.9%
2005	21.0%	16.8%	11.4%	5.7%	5.8%	7.3%	-3.9%
2006	25.0%	11.5%	7.4%	6.0%	3.1%	4.1%	2.4%
2007	18.0%	-2.6%	-5.3%	6.8%	3.5%	7.0%	11.7%
2008	-40.4%	-24.9%	-19.8%	7.6%	15.0%	13.4%	-7.7%
2009	39.6%	-0.3%	-2.3%	3.5%	1.7%	4.0%	15.5%
2010	3.3%	-2.0%	1.5%	4.7%	6.0%	8.3%	8.1%
2011	-11.4%	-5.3%	2.2%	5.0%	11.4%	10.8%	-4.4%
2012	18.8%	14.1%	13.5%	4.0%	7.7%	8.4%	2.0%
2013	19.7%	48.0%	53.6%	2.9%	2.0%	2.5%	13.9%
2014	5.0%	15.0%	24.0%	2.7%	9.8%	11.0%	9.3%
2015	3.8%	11.8%	13.8%	2.3%	2.6%	3.8%	11.0%
2016	11.6%	7.9%	13.0%	2.1%	2.9%	5.2%	12.4%

▓ Asset class with highest return for the year; ▓ Asset class with the lowest return for the year.

Source: Data from www.vanguardinvestments.com.au supplied by Andex Charts Pty Ltd.
Residential property is the change in the average median house price in Melbourne and Sydney supplied by REIA.

monkeys. After 100 contests, the *Wall Street Journal* presented the results, which showed the experts won 61 of the contests and the dart throwers won 39. However, the experts were only able to beat the Dow Jones Industrial Average (DJIA) in 51 contests. Malkiel commented that the experts' picks were aided by the publicity jump in the price of a stock that tends to occur when stock experts make a recommendation.

In summary, a dart board almost does just as good a job at predicting returns as what professionals do. I suggest you adopt the belief (or agreement) that returns are random and no-one can predict them. If you invest accordingly, you will likely be better off in the long run.

A list of the different asset classes

So now that we know a bit more about asset allocation and the randomness of short-term returns, let's look at the different asset classes you might choose to invest in. The major asset classes include:

- *Shares*, including domestic (Australian) and international.

- *Bonds*, including domestic and international. The three main categories of bonds are government, corporate and mortgage-backed.

- *Cash*, including high-yielding at-call accounts, cash at bank and term deposits.

- *Property*, which may include commercial and residential direct property.

Note that I do not regard listed property trusts (often called 'real estate investment trusts' or 'REITs') as a perfect proxy for owning direct property, for two reasons. Firstly, one of the benefits of owning direct property is that you have full control over the asset (you have little to no control over the property owned by a REIT). Secondly, REITs start behaving more like equities in that expectations and market sentiment can influence their value/prices. Where possible, always opt for holding direct property.

As well as those asset classes in the preceding list, alternative asset classes are available. These tend to be higher risk and, typically, I would advise my clients not to invest any more than 5 per cent of their overall wealth in these assets. Alternative asset classes include:

- *Commodities*, including oil, gas and gold – you can normally get access to these in a low-cost, diversified way using an ETF (see Golden Rule #6).

- *Private equity*, such as through investing in an unlisted business.

- *Hedge funds*, which are actively managed investments that use higher risk strategies (such as derivatives, leverage and short-selling) to generate higher returns.

- *Artwork and collectables.*

- *Small cap stocks.*

I've included small cap stocks in the preceding list because, while this is not strictly an alternative asset class (it is more correctly a sub-set of the 'shares' asset class), I do regard it as an alternative. Small cap investments consist of investing in listed businesses with a market capitalisation (value) on the ASX of less than $200 million to $400 million (in other words, stocks outside of the ASX200). These investments typically exhibit much higher risk (volatility). I discuss this aspect of volatility in the following section.

Volatility and its impact on returns

The volatility of an investment refers to the likelihood of the investment returns varying from their mean (average). A highly volatile investment is one where its returns vary wildly from one year to the next. A low volatility investment provides stable and consistent investment returns. Volatility can be measured at an asset level and at a portfolio level. Your aim should be to structure your portfolio in such a way that it has a low volatility. This typically means you will hold a mixture of high volatility assets and low volatility assets.

Volatility can have a significant impact on your investment returns – something that is perhaps best explained using an example. Assume that you invest $100,000 in a (quite volatile) share market managed fund. The following table outlines the returns over five years for this example fund.

Year	Return	Investment balance
Year 0		$100,000
Year 1	–22%	$78,000
Year 2	2%	$79,560
Year 3	40%	$111,384
Year 4	–10%	$100,246
Year 5	25%	$125,307
Average return	**7%**	**Compound return = 4.6%**

The average return over the five years is 7.0 per cent p.a. (To determine this figure, simply add up the five years of returns and divide by five.) However, the *compound* (geometric) annual return is only 4.6 per cent p.a. over the five-year period. The compound return is the average annual return you would need to earn to increase your investment from $100,000 to $125,307 after five years.

Notice that the average return is higher than the compound return. The reason for this is that the losses and large volatility (variance) in returns dramatically reduced the investor's balance.

If you have $100 and lose 50 per cent, you will have $50. If you make 50 per cent back the following year, you will have $75 – still less than the $100 you started with! So, you need to make a 100 per cent return just to get back to where you started. That is why Benjamin Graham taught Warren Buffett how important it is to invest in a manner so that you *almost never lose money*. (Remember Graham's two rules to investing. The first rule was to 'never lose money'. The second rule was to 'refer to rule number one'.)

The volatility of an investment is a good proxy for its 'risk' – that is, the higher the volatility, the riskier an investment is.

The historical risk of different asset classes (volatility)

The following chart plots the historical volatility of various asset classes over a 36-year period (1980 to 2016) in comparison to their long-term returns. You will note that shares have a volatility of between 20 and 25 per cent p.a. and a return of between 10 and 13 per cent p.a. Direct (Australian) residential property has a historical return and volatility of approximately 10 per cent p.a. Bonds have a historical return and volatility of between 8 per cent and 9 per cent p.a.[1]

What does this all mean? It means that, given Australian shares have an average return of around 11 per cent p.a. and a volatility of around 21 per cent p.a., you can expect that if you invest in Australian shares, your annual investment returns are likely to be in the range of negative 10 per cent and positive 32 per cent (big range, hey!).

Asset class returns and volatility between 1980 and 2016

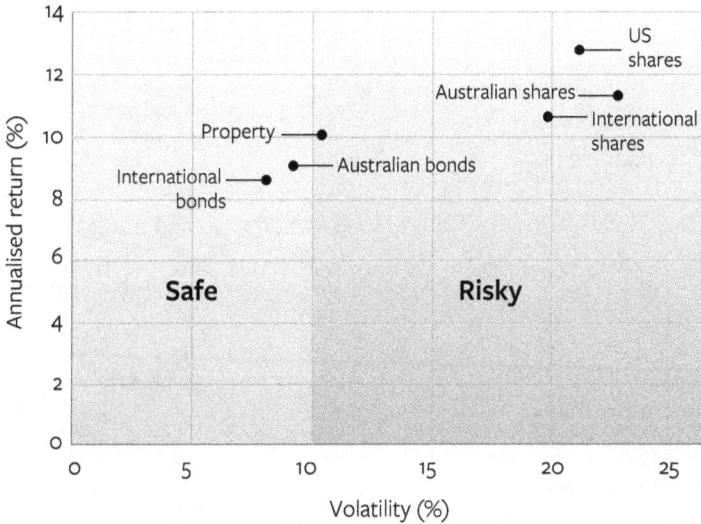

Data supplied by Andex Charts Pty Ltd & REIA. Australian shares = S&P/ASX All Ordinaries Accumulation Index; International shares = MSCI World ex-Australia Net Total Return Index; US shares = S&P 500 Total Return Index. Australian property = average median house price of Sydney and Melbourne plus 2 per cent for net rental income. Australian Bonds = UBS Warburg Australia Composite Bond Accumulation Index; International Bonds = Barclays Capital Global Treasury Index (AUD hedged).

The following tables illustrate these trends further, showing the historical investment returns and volatility over 36, 26 and 16 years for various asset classes. The biggest 'take away' from this data is that returns are random, but volatility is comparatively predictable. Volatility rarely changes. This will help you in your decision of how much to invest in each asset class, because you know which asset classes exhibit the highest risk.

Asset class returns and volatility between 1980 and 2016: 36 years

Asset class	Volatility/risk	Annualised return
US shares	21.05%	12.81%
International shares	19.82%	10.66%
Australian shares	21.74%	11.34%
Australian property	10.14%	10.07%
Australian bonds	9.13%	9.10%
International bonds	8.24%	8.62%

Asset class returns and volatility between 1990 and 2016: 26 years

Asset class	Volatility/risk	Annualised return
US shares	20.51%	9.75%
International shares	17.83%	6.42%
Australian shares	17.80%	9.09%
Australian property	7.40%	8.68%
Australian bonds	6.99%	8.12%
International bonds	5.36%	8.45%

Asset class returns and volatility between 2000 and 2016: 16 years

Asset class	Volatility/risk	Annualised return
US shares	17.93%	3.88%
International shares	17.65%	2.43%
Australian shares	17.66%	7.90%
Australian property	7.86%	8.62%
Australian bonds	5.04%	6.27%
International Bonds	3.63%	7.50%

Source for all three tables: Data supplied by Andex Charts Pty Ltd & REIA. Australian shares = S&P/ASX All Ordinaries Accumulation Index; International shares = MSCI World ex-Australia Net Total Return Index; US shares = S&P 500 Total Return Index. Australian property = average median house price of Sydney and Melbourne plus 2 per cent for net rental income. Australian Bonds = UBS Warburg Australia Composite Bond Accumulation Index; International Bonds = Barclays Capital Global Treasury Index (AUD hedged).

An important warning about discounting any one asset class

You might look at the data shown in the preceding tables and figure and conclude that you should only invest in direct property and bonds – forget about shares! I believe that you should only invest in assets that you are 100 per cent comfortable with – so don't force yourself to invest in assets that make you feel uncomfortable. However, please do me one favour. Please don't make a decision about your willingness to invest in property or shares until you read Golden Rules #6 and #7. Keep an open mind, read these chapters first and then decide.

Asset allocation according to risk

Given that we now know that shares are three times riskier than bonds, this helps us look at an asset allocation differently. For example, if 50 per cent of your money is invested in shares and 50 per cent in bonds, you might feel that you have a 'low-risk' asset allocation. However, the risk is not spread 50/50 if stocks are three times riskier than bonds. In fact, according to Tony Robbins's book *Money: Mastering the Game*, which looks at historical returns between 1973 and 2013 in the US, a 50/50 portfolio really has a risk allocation of 95 per cent from the shares component and 5 per cent from bonds.

Portfolio construction: combine assets with negative correlations

Volatility is only half of the story, so now let's look at the other half: correlation. Correlation refers to how one asset behaves when a different asset changes in value. A negative correlation means that when one asset increases in value, the other falls.

The role of your asset allocation is to invest in a way so that you make money no matter what happens – that way, you don't need to worry about whether the stock market is up or down, for example.

The best way to do this is to invest in assets that are negatively correlated. The following table sets out the correlation between various asset classes.

Asset classes	Correlation
International shares versus US shares	90%
Australian shares versus international shares	61%
Australian shares versus US shares	43%
Australian shares versus Australian bonds	–16%
Australian residential property versus Australian shares	20%
Australian residential property versus Australian bonds	–23%
Australian residential property versus international bonds	–15
Australian residential property versus international shares	2%

Source data covering the period 1980 to 2016 supplied by Andex Charts Pty Ltd & REIA. Australian shares = S&P/ASX All Ordinaries Accumulation Index; International shares = MSCI World ex-Australia Net Total Return Index; US shares = S&P 500 Total Return Index. Australian residential property = average median house price of Sydney and Melbourne plus 2 per cent for net rental income. Australian Bonds = UBS Warburg Australia Composite Bond Accumulation Index; International Bonds = Barclays Capital Global Treasury Index (AUD hedged).

How to read the table: A 100 per cent correlation represents a perfect correlation – so if one asset's value appreciates by 2 per cent, the other asset's value will appreciate by the same amount. A correlation of minus 100 per cent represents a perfectly negative correlation – so if one asset's value appreciates by

2 per cent, the other asset's value will depreciate by 2 per cent. And a zero per cent correlation means that no relationship exists between the two asset classes (no correlation).

As you can see, bonds have a negative correlation with Australian property and shares. Australian shares have a positive correlation with international shares and with US shares to a lesser extent. Virtually no correlation exists between Australian property and international shares, and a very weak positive correlation exists with Australian shares.

We can glean a few key observations from this data:

- Bonds (and cash) have a negative correlation to residential property and shares.

- US and international shares have an almost perfect positive correlation and therefore should be considered the 'same' when developing an asset allocation (which is not surprising, given the US market constitutes circa 60 per cent of the international index).

- Australian residential property has a very weak correlation with most other asset classes.

Therefore, to achieve correlation diversification, most investors will benefit from investing in:

- Some bonds, cash and fixed-interest investments

- Some Australian shares

- Some international and US shares

- Some direct residential property.

A portfolio that includes negatively correlated assets will have some winners and some losers (in terms of investment returns) at any given time. Over time, the aim is that the wins more than offset the losses to produce a positive overall return at a portfolio level. As a result, the portfolio's overall volatility should be relatively low.

How much do you put in each asset class?

So far in this chapter we have discussed that returns are random and that some asset classes are a lot riskier than others (due to volatility). We have also covered the benefit of investing in assets that are negatively correlated (or have no correlation). At this point, you are probably thinking, *This is great but what does it all mean? How do I work out how much money to put into each asset class?* The answer to these questions is part art and part science.

You need to consider many things when determining the best asset allocation for your situation. However, the most important considerations include:

- *Your investment time horizon:* This relates to the amount of time you're able to invest for before you need the monies. You need to consider two points of time here. The first one is the number of years until you would like to retire – for example, the number of years you are away from turning 60. The second is the number of years until death. This is important because, if you assume that you will retire at age 60 and live to age 90, then you don't want to invest too defensively (conservatively) at age 60 – otherwise, you might run out of money. The longer the investment time horizon, the greater the capacity you have to accept higher risk (volatility) so that you can capture a higher return.

- *Your need to draw income and capital:* Different asset classes deliver different proportions of capital growth and income.

For example, direct property typically provides 20 per cent of its total return in income and 80 per cent in capital growth. International shares provide similar percentages to property – with maybe slightly more income. Australian shares will typically provide 50 per cent in income and in capital growth. And bonds and fixed-interest securities provide most of their return in income. If you are nearing (or in) retirement, you might have to tilt your asset allocation towards more income-style assets.

• *Your risk appetite:* How often are you willing to risk a negative return? Once every 20 years? Or a couple of times in a decade? Do you have the stomach to withstand a loss of 30 to 40 per cent in any one year (as shares can sometimes do)? And is your financial position strong enough to be able to afford to take such risks? Answers to questions like these will help determine your capacity and willingness to take on investment risk. If you are risk averse, you should invest most of your assets in 'safe' asset classes (see the chart provided earlier in this chapter for examples of these). For further help with measuring and understanding your risk profile, I have provided a link to an excellent (and quick) risk tolerance questionnaire at www.investopoly.com.au.

Don't forget the impact of the bond bull market

Bond markets in the 1980s and, to a lesser extent, the 1990s performed very well. In Australia and the US, for example, government bond investment returns typically ranged from 12 to 14 per cent p.a. in the 1980s. Since the GFC, government bond returns in Australia particularly have been gradually declining and are pretty flat. Meanwhile, the US has been experiencing higher than usual volatility in the past decade.

We need to take this into account when considering the historical returns for bonds. In the long run, I think it is reasonable to expect a bond portfolio to generate investment returns in the range of 4.50 to 6.50 per cent p.a. – which is in line with longer term returns dating back to the 1920s (that is, excluding the bull market already mentioned). Put differently, I think it is unrealistic to expect another bond bull market like what was experienced in the 1980s and 1990s. Therefore, when calculating various portfolio returns in the following sections, I have provided the 'actual' return and an 'adjusted' return – in which I have adjusted bond returns to what I believe to be a more normalised level.

Example asset allocation approaches

When developing a strategic asset allocation, a few different approaches are possible:

- *Calculate 100 minus your age:* This equals the percentage of growth (that is, risky) assets you should hold. For example, if you are 80, only 20 per cent of your assets should be invested in growth assets. If you are 30, on the other hand, 70 per cent of your monies should be invested in growth assets. This is an old rule of thumb, and some commentators have suggested the number should be changed from 100 to 120 – to account for lower than expected bond returns.

- *Allocate in the range of 70 to 80 per cent of your wealth into 'risky' assets:* This is a common 'growth' asset allocation that is typically appropriate for investors in their forties or younger.

- *Use the 'All Weather Portfolio' allocation:* This allocation mix was developed by Ray Dalio, arguably the world's most successful hedge fund manager. Dalio uses this mix to manage his clients' monies (his hedge fund is called Bridgewater and his institutional clients invest an average of $500 million each). This 'all weather' allocation includes 30 per cent invested in stocks, 40 per cent in long-term government bonds, 15 per cent in medium-term government bonds (7- to 10-year securities), 7.5 per cent in gold and 7.5 per cent in commodities. Tony Robbins discusses this asset allocation in *Money: Mastering the Game*, highlighting it has generated a return of 9.60 per cent p.a. over the past 30 years – with low volatility. Of course, a large driver of this performance is the bond bull market discussed in the previous section.

Back-testing different asset allocations

Using the appropriate indexes (see Golden Rule #6 for more on this) and median property prices in Melbourne and Sydney, I have calculated how different asset allocations have performed over the 36 years from January 1980 through to December 2016. The results for these asset allocations are listed in the following sections.

Of course, past performance is not necessarily a reliable indicator of future performance. However, these historical results should give you a good sense of what returns you might be able to expect and the volatility (risk) of different asset allocations.[2]

A very conservative asset allocation

The following table shows historical returns for a very conservative asset allocation focusing on cash and bonds.

1980–2016: 10% cash, 45% Australian bonds,
45% international bonds

	Actual historical results	Adjusted bond results
Compound annual return	8.87%	6.20%
Number of loss years	2	0
Maximum return	23.32%	15.03%
Minimum return	–3.02%	2.02%
Volatility	6.14%	3.22%

Allocation with no property

The next table shows results if the asset allocation focused all invested monies in bonds, cash and shares – that is, with no direct residential property.

1980–2016: 35% Australian shares, 15% US shares, 15% international shares, 10% cash, 12.5% Australian bonds, 12.5% international bonds

	Actual historical results	Adjusted bond results
Compound annual return	11.22%	10.49%
Number of loss years	6	6
Maximum return	40.70%	37.53%
Minimum return	–16.54%	–17.64%
Volatility	12.35%	11.80%

Allocation with mostly property

Now let's see the results for an asset allocation that assumes a strong preference for investing in direct residential property and a lower allocation in shares – this might be the case if, say, the only share investments you have are within your super.

1980–2016: 20% Australian shares, 10% US shares, 5% international shares, 5% cash, 7.5% Australian bonds, 7.5% international bonds, 45% residential property

	Actual historical results	Adjusted bond results
Compound annual return	10.86%	10.41%
Number of loss years	4	3
Maximum return	28.11%	26.42%
Minimum return	–10.00%	–10.66%
Volatility	8.46%	8.28%

A balanced approach

The final table shows results from an asset allocation that assumed a balanced approach – that is, not favouring any one asset class. If following this asset allocation now, it is best achieved by investing in property in the early stages of your investment journey and then complementing super with some additional share investments (after the property assets have been acquired).

1980–2016: 20% Australian shares, 12.5% US shares, 7.5% international shares, 5% cash, 10% Australian bonds, 10% international bonds, 35% residential property

	Actual historical results	Adjusted bond results
Compound annual return	10.93%	10.33%
Number of loss years	5	3
Maximum return	29.64%	27.10%
Minimum return	–10.20%	–11.08%
Volatility	8.66%	8.32%

As you can see from the preceding tables, if you invest too conservatively, your return will be a lot lower. Therefore, you must invest in some risky assets to generate a higher return. Typically, the best approach is a diversified one because it generates virtually the same return with lower volatility.

Small tactical tilts

Assuming the balanced allocation suits you best, you should invest around 20 per cent of your overall wealth in Australian shares. However, as mentioned, you can still make slight adjustments to this allocation, depending on your view of current market conditions. If you hold the view that the Australian market is undervalued for example, you might invest such that you are overweight in Australian shares – investing, say, 22 per cent of your wealth into this asset class. This is how a strategic asset allocation interacts with a tactical one. You must have the discipline to stick to a diversified strategic asset allocation while still having some flexibility to make small changes.

> *I think that the first thing is you should have a strategic asset allocation mix that assumes that you don't know what the future is going to hold.*
>
> Ray Dalio

Golden Rule #5 summary

In this chapter we discussed:

- Asset allocation is important because it determines what returns, risk and volatility you will likely experience as an investor.

- Adopting a strategic asset allocation is best, and then making small tactical tilts to accommodate market conditions.

- Investment returns are random and, therefore, inherently unpredictable. A dart board can do almost as good a job predicting returns as seasoned professionals.

- The main asset classes to consider are shares, property, bonds and cash.

- Volatility is a measure of risk. You should aim to reduce risk (volatility) by investing in a combination of assets – in other words, having a finger in every pie.

- Investment returns over various periods can differ significantly. However, asset class validity rarely differs – it is relatively constant.

- You need to construct a portfolio of negatively correlated assets so that in any one year you will have some winners and some losers. Over time, the wins should more than outweigh the losses to result in a positive return.

- To develop an asset allocation for yourself, you need to consider your investment time horizon, the amount of income and capital gains you need, and your risk profile.

- Back-testing various asset allocations showed their results over the past 36 years, including their relative volatility.

Note you must get the methodology correct to achieve historical returns

It is all very well to be happy to invest in various asset classes, but it is critically important that you select an investment methodology or approach that gives you the best possible chance of winning (that is, generating good returns with low volatility). This is what the following two golden rules focus on. I will share with you how to successfully invest in residential property, and share and bond markets so that you have a very high probability of achieving (or beating) the historical returns noted in this chapter.

---

1   A recent academic paper produced very similar results to mine – see Òscar Jordà, Katherine Knoll, Dmitry Kuvshinov, Moritz Schularisk and Alan M Taylor, 2017, 'The Rate of Return on Everything 1870–2015', Federal Reserve Bank of San Francisco Working Paper 2017-25.

2   In the results listed, I produced a series of synthetic bond returns that essentially reduced the average bond return from 9 per cent p.a. over the past 36 years to 6 per cent p.a., to reduce the impact of the bond bull market in the 1980s and 1990s.

INVEST IN THE SHARE MARKET USING A LOW-COST PASSIVE INVESTMENT METHODOLOGY

Most share market investors, professionals and novices alike, produce poor investment returns. The reason for this poor performance is almost always because the share investment methodology they have chosen is flawed – or, worse, there's a complete absence of methodology.

This chapter sets out an evidenced-based share investing methodology that has strong roots in academia. No longer do you have to put your faith in a share market 'oracle' and/or pay high fees to an advisor. Indeed, you can avoid stock picking and actively managed funds altogether. Instead, you can invest in the share market (including your super) using a very low-cost, rules-based approach that has been proven to produce superior returns.

Perhaps you don't feel comfortable with investing in the share market because you don't understand it or have lost money in the past. Either way, put any preconceived preferences aside for a moment and read this chapter with an open mind. The methodology I provide here is easy-to-understand and makes sense. But first, let's look at some of the myths that still exist around share investing, and how my approach differs from these ideas.

Disproving some myths about share investing

For most things in life, our opinions and views are shaped by our environment and past experiences. Share investing is no different. A lot of people view share investing as risky, for example, and don't think they can consistently make money by investing in shares.

One of the common concerns with share investing is the lack of 'physicality' – for example, if you own stocks in a company that doesn't have a lot of hard assets and its value is instead represented by goodwill, intellectual property and so on, its value can be very subjective. This is quite different from residential property, which is a hard or physical asset with a lot less subjectivity involved in valuing it.

Another common concern is the complexity involved in understanding and monitoring the share market. Novice investors think that investing in the share market requires them to pick individual stocks and follow those stocks on a daily basis. Few people have the time and inclination to do this. As such, they discount investing in shares as an option.

While some of these concerns might have an element of truth, my aim with this chapter is to demonstrate to you that you can actually invest in shares in a very transparent and low-risk manner. In fact, I would like to demonstrate to you that investing in shares:

- is easy to understand and simple to execute

- is relatively low risk if done correctly

- can be quite 'set and forget' – will only take a few hours a year

- can achieve broadly the same investment returns as other major growth asset classes.

Four common share investing mistakes

Share investing hasn't worked for many people because they have repeated the same four simple mistakes. Nearly every novice investor I meet has made these same mistakes. The shame is that these mistakes are so easy to avoid.

Before I cover these common mistakes, let's have a quick look at some observations. When I meet a client who has invested in a direct share portfolio (either personally or in an SMSF), 95 per cent of the time I typically find the following:

- The investor's overall investment returns are ordinary at best. Typically, the investor has not made any money or has lost money (the portfolio is in a break-even or loss position). Almost always, the investor has also not tracked or benchmarked their investments' performance. Again, you can only manage what you measure – so if you are investing in direct shares and not benchmarking yourself to the index, you are setting yourself up to fail!

- The portfolio usually consists of approximately 20 or fewer stocks. Further, they are usually all Australian businesses (listed on the ASX). Rarely does the investor have any international exposure.

- Only one or two (of the 20 selected) stocks are in a profit position. The remaining 18 are either at break-even or loss positions.

- Whether the investor has used a broker, share investing newsletter or nothing at all doesn't seem to have had any influence on their investment success (or lack thereof).

As mentioned, these poor returns are caused by making four common mistakes, covered in the following sections.

Mistake #1: The absence of a methodology

Most unsuccessful investors do not adopt and follow an investment methodology or strategy. Instead, they tend to make very ad hoc investment decisions. This absence of strategy then leaves investment returns to mere chance or luck.

In some cases, investors might have a strategy or reason for investing in particular stocks. However, in terms of the way they invest and their overall asset allocation, their approach still tends to be very ad hoc.

Could you imagine an AFL coach not preparing a game plan? (Okay, one would be forgiven for concluding that Collingwood do this regularly.) Thinking through a methodology or strategy allows you to consider how you will win at the investing game before you even invest one cent. If you're not prepared to develop a strategy, my advice is not to waste your time investing. Again, it would be like building a house without architectural plans. It's that important.

Mistake #2: A belief they can make quick profits

Here I'd like to repeat probably my all-time favourite quote (from Howard Schultz, who built Starbucks): 'Short-term profit does not create long-term value for anyone'. It is very true. Stock market investors who chase short-term profits almost always don't generating long-term value.

In the stock market, for every winner, there must be a loser on the other side of the transaction – just as there is a seller for every buyer. If you buy a stock today because you formed the view that it was undervalued or would grow in the future, the person who sold the stock to you is likely to have held the contrary view. And maybe that person had far more experience and education than you?

Who do you think the loser is going to be? The novice investor who enjoys share market investing as a 'hobby'? Or the professional fund managers with teams of smart people who study the market 80 hours a week? Or the supercomputer with artificial intelligence that makes high frequency trades every millisecond to exploit small arbitrage opportunities?

A far better approach is to invest for long-term value. As Warren Buffett advises, 'Only buy something that you'd be perfectly happy to hold if the market shut down for 10 years'. I believe this is an excellent 'acid test' for any investment asset class.

Mistake #3: No patience

Share 'trading' (which is different from share 'investing') can be an expensive business – one that generates expenses (share brokerage) and tax consequences. Notwithstanding that, to be successful, you have to keep coming up with winning ideas, consistently. It's a lot of work and has a very low success rate.

Whereas, if you invested $10,000 in CBA when it floated at $5.40 per share in 1991, your investment would be worth approximately $150,000 at the time of writing (December 2017) – not including any dividend income (and if dividends were reinvested, your investment would be worth significantly more). To quote Buffett again, 'the stock market has a very efficient way of transferring wealth from the impatient to the patient'.

Mistake #4: Almost no diversification

Most of the investment portfolios that I review are invested almost entirely in the big four banks, CSL, BHP and Telstra. They lack a lot of diversification and often have no exposure to certain sectors such as technology.

The Australian stock market is inherently concentrated (that is, it lacks diversification). The top five stocks make up over 25 per cent of the S&P/ASX 200 index – and half of the index's value lies in only 13 stocks. Financial stocks make up 35 per cent, materials 17 per cent and technology a lonely 1.3 per cent. This means that even if you do invest in an S&P/ASX 200 index fund, you still won't have achieved much in the way of diversification.

Take technology for an example. Some of the biggest tech companies in the world include Apple, Google, Microsoft, Facebook, Samsung, Oracle and Intel. It is reasonable to assume these companies will make a significant contribution to the world economy over the next 10 to 30 years. And, therefore, not having any exposure to them would be foolhardy from an investment perspective.

In short, it's very difficult to achieve any meaningful diversification (to reduce unsystematic risk) with a portfolio of only 20 ASX-listed shares.

The marketing story that has cost investors billions!

> *Most advisors, however, are far better at generating high fees than they are at generating high returns. In truth, their core competence is salesmanship.*
>
> Warren Buffett, in a 2014 letter to shareholders

Everyone likes an 'insider's tip', don't they – something that gives them the edge over everyone else? So, if I told you that I have this awesome investment methodology that allows me to make money in the stock market and it can't fail, you might be interested, right? Most people would be, and this is how the financial services industry has successfully marketed itself for many decades. I mean it's a great story to tell, isn't it? 'Pay me a fee and I'll make you lots of money. I am the expert so that's why you can't do it without me. I can invest your money better than you can.'

However, this story is nothing more than a marketing tactic. Let me tell you why. Generally, two methodologies are used to invest money: either *active* or *passive*. Here's how each of these methodologies works:

1. Active fund managers try to beat the market by deciding what stocks to invest in. (This type of funds management is probably what you are familiar with.) These fund managers typically choose from two approaches – value and/or growth. A *value* approach means that they will buy stock that they think is undervalued in the hope that the market will eventually value them correctly (assuming the fund manager's assessment of value is correct). A *growth* approach involves investing in companies which, in the investment manager's opinion, have great growth prospects that they hope will be reflected in their future share price growth. Active fund managers typically charge in the range of 1 to 2.5 per cent p.a. in fees.

2. A passive (or index-based) approach is based on the philosophy that you can't beat the market because the participants are highly skilled and the market is efficient. Instead, you should invest in an index fund – such as one based on the S&P/ASX 200, for example. An S&P/ASX 200

index fund will invest in the top 200 companies weighted by their market capitalisation (value). In December 2017 (as I write this chapter), CBA makes up 8.11 per cent of the index so, if following this strategy, 8.11 per cent of your money would be invested in CBA. Index funds charge in the range of 0.04 to 0.40 per cent p.a. in fees, depending upon the methodology used.

The goal of the non-professional should not be to pick winners – neither he nor his 'helpers' can do that – but should rather be to own a cross-section of businesses that in aggregate are bound to do well. A low-cost S&P 500 index fund will achieve this goal.

Warren Buffett, in a 2014 letter to shareholders

Passive has a higher probability of generating higher returns in the long run

The big difference between passive and active investment methodologies is how they have performed over the long term.

In the mid-1970s, Burton Malkiel and Jack Bogle started the 'passive investing' revolution. They co-founded Vanguard, a not-for-profit investment manager, largely off the back of Malkiel's bestselling book *A Random Walk Down Wall Street* (which has sold millions of copies and is in its 11th edition). As discussed in Golden Rule #5, the thesis behind Malkiel's book was that returns are random, and no-one can consistently pick winners. In fact, he uses the analogy that trying to pick a winning stock is akin to finding a needle in a haystack. He suggests that instead of trying to find the needle in the haystack, just invest in the haystack (in other words, the index).

A huge (and still growing) body of research supports Malkiel and Bogle's hypothesis. This research shows that while some active fund managers can beat the market one or two years in a row, very few (virtually none) can beat the market consistently year on year over the long term – for example, over a decade or more. In addition, when you take into account that active fund managers charge significantly higher fees than passive fund managers, their performance looks even worse. Knowing this, the challenge then becomes how do you consistently pick which active fund manager will beat the market over the next 12 months? And how will you be able to consistently pick when said fund manager's performance will deteriorate (so you can switch to the next high-performing manager)? The simple answer is that virtually no-one has developed a consistent and reliable methodology to achieve this. As such, the conclusion in all this research is that investors are better off investing passively (in index funds).

Here is a summary of some of the research that has been completed:

- The SPIVA® Scorecard produced by S&P Dow Jones Indices (updated twice per year) calculates how many active funds have outperformed the market in the past five years. Based on the most recent data (ending June 2017), only 35 per cent of active funds in Australia and 18 per cent in the US beat the index in the past five years (more about why this might be in the following section). You can find a link to the latest results at www.investopoly.com.au.

- Industry expert Robert Arnott, founder of US-based firm Research Affiliates, spent two decades studying the top 200 active US fund managers with at least $100 million under management. He concluded that from 1984 to 1998, a full 15 years, only eight out of 200 fund managers beat the Vanguard 500 Index. That is, 96 per cent of active fund managers failed to beat the market over this 15-year period.

- The median Australian active manager's return (after fees) for the five years to 2006 was 13.7 per cent. The S&P/ASX 300 index's return for the same period was 15.9 per cent. That said, the five years to 2006 made up a very strong bull market. Theoretically, active managers' skills should be more obvious in a falling market because, let's face it, anyone can make money in a rising market. So let's look at the year ended 30 June 2008. The median active fund manager lost 14.05 per cent for this year compared to the S&P/ASX 200's loss of 13.75 per cent over the same period according to Mercer (after adjusting for fees per Morningstar).

And here's a quick summary of other studies:

- In his 1991 article 'The Arithmetic of Active Management', William Sharpe suggests that active management will result in more frequent trading and higher research costs than passive management.

- In *3 Guaranteed Ways to Improve Your Portfolio and Pensions* from 2008, author Rob Noble-Warren notes Burton Malkiel's findings that 70 per cent of all active equity managers underperform the returns of the S&P 500 Index.

- In his 'Mutual Fund Performance' article from 2000, Russ Wermers finds that while equity mutual funds do outperform the market index, once expenses and transaction costs are taken into account they are equivalent in performance.

- In the article 'How Mutual Funds Lost Their Way', published in 2000 in the *Wall Street Journal*, John Bogle from Vanguard finds index funds outperform the average equity mutual fund because of the lower management and brokerage costs, sales charges and tax advantages associated with the index funds.

- In 'The Management and Mismanagement of Taxable Assets' from 2000, Robert Arnott, Andrew Berkin and Jia Ye find that the Vanguard 500 Index Fund outperforms the average equity fund.

- In the article 'Indexing versus Active Mutual Fund Management' from 2002, Rich Fortin and Stuart Michelson find that, on average, index funds outperform actively managed mutual funds for most equity and all bond funds.

This is only a selection of research. They have not been cherry picked. You can do your own research via Google. I'm confident that you'll find the theme is overwhelmingly supportive of the fact that evidence suggests indexing is better than active.

Top performers don't stay at the top for long

If you do happen to find an actively managed fund that has outperformed the market (net of their fees), research suggests that the 'outperformance' won't persist for very long. The research provided by S&P Dow Jones Indices in 'Does Past Performance Matter? The Persistence Scorecard' from 2017 demonstrated that of the fund managers that were in the top quartile as of March 2015 (performance wise), only 1.94 per cent managed to remain in the top quartile by the end of March 2017. That is, only a tiny number of funds can consistently stay at the top year after year.

Two conclusions from all this research

The best way I can summarise all the research into active versus passive investment is with the following:

1. The research shows that if we pick an actively managed fund and invest with it for the long term, a tiny chance exists that we will beat the index (around 4 per cent).

2. Therefore, the challenge then becomes that we need to pick which fund manager will beat the index in the short run and then somehow predict when we should sack that fund manager and move to the next potential winner. However, since very few active managers do beat the index (35 per cent in Australia and 18 per cent in the US), this is a very difficult process. The odds are heavily stacked against us.

In short, this is a loser's game!

So why would you ever invest in active funds, especially given their fees are in the range of 3 to 20 times more expensive?

Why the industry is fighting it

As you can imagine, the investment management and commission-based financial planning industries haven't embraced these research findings. Of course, these industries have a lot of money to lose if investors stop believing the fees they charge represent good value for money. These industries – including the large super funds – have relied upon the 'marketing story' that suggests these high active management and advice fees are, in fact, very worthwhile. Unfortunately, the research findings rebut that notion.

Now, it would be silly for me to conclude that no-one can beat the market consistently. A select few fund managers have, of course, actually beaten the market over the long term (this includes Warren Buffett, Ray Dalio and David Swensen, to name a few) – but they are the top 0.0001 per cent of investors in the world. We don't have the same chance when we invest in the same market as these guys. Actively investing in the share market is like playing poker against the World Series of Poker champion ... you stand a very slim a chance of winning.

Passive in Australia versus the rest of the world

Most of the studies comparing passive and active investment strategies have focused on the US stock market. This makes a lot of sense given their market is significantly larger than Australia's and they have more historical data. So when reading this research, you have a few important local considerations:

- The Australian market lacks a lot of diversification (as discussed earlier in this chapter). Arguably, this means an active fund manager should be able to more easily beat the index because the index is mainly driven by the performance of the top 10 companies. Therefore, an active fund manager only needs to form a view on the future performance of these 10 companies and, if the passage of time proves their view to be correct, they will beat the index. Having said that, around 70 per cent of Australian active fund managers still fail to beat the index.

- A recent phenomenon is that Australian active fund managers have become so worried about not beating index (and suffering the resultant bad press) that their investment holdings (that is, the stocks they're investing in) start to closely replicate the index. This is called 'index hugging'. As such, the people who invest in these funds are paying very high fees for a product that is essentially an index fund.

- Looking at the data from the SPIVA® Australia Scorecard, it appears that active fund managers perform slightly better in a flat market compared to a rising market. (The SPIVA Scorecard reports on the performance of actively managed Australian funds against their respective benchmark indices over specific investment time frames.) Therefore, when looking at the data (especially for shorter terms such as one and three years) you should consider the prevailing market conditions over that period of time.

Investors (big and small) are mass-exiting active investments

According to Morningstar, in the year to August 2017, over $US200 billion flowed out (net) of active funds management in the US. By comparison, over the same period, almost $700 billion flowed into passive funds (net). This overwhelmingly demonstrates that investors in the US are voting with their feet. The transition away from active funds management towards passive management is gaining more momentum with each year that passes.

The same is occurring in Australia, albeit at a slightly reduced rate compared to the US. Over the past 10 years, the exchange traded funds (ETFs) market has grown at a compounding rate of more than 40 per cent per year. (ETFs are almost always passively managed investments.) The difference in adoption between the US and Australian markets is that institutional investors (large corporations) in the US use passive investments more than their counterparts in Australia. In other words, Australian institutions have been slower to adopt a passive style of investing. In my opinion, Australian industry super funds should be leading the way in this but, unfortunately, they're not. That said, it's only a matter of time because more of their members will start demanding quality passive investment options.

Three other advantages of passive investing

Apart from their performance in terms of returns, passive or index funds have other advantages – including lower fees, reduced tax and other costs and increased diversification.

Lower fees

Future returns – from active or passive funds – are uncertain, whereas the fees you pay are guaranteed. The fund manager will take their fees irrespective of the investment's performance. Therefore, one school of thought is that you should minimise investment fees as much as possible.

According to S&P Dow Jones Indices, the average Australian management fee being charged by active managers in 2016 was 1.24 per cent p.a., versus just 0.33 per cent p.a. charged by passive funds. (I discuss the impact fees have on your investment balance later in this chapter.)

Adopting a passive investment strategy alleviates the need to spend time, energy and money trying to pick winning fund managers and/or individual stocks. If you do engage the services of a financial advisor, arguably the fees they charge you will be reduced because they don't need to spend any time on stock and fund manager selection. The main things a financial advisor needs to focus on (with a passive investment strategy) are your asset allocation and reviewing, updating and adopting any new passive investment strategies.

Reduced turnover means lower tax and costs

Many active funds trade stocks a lot more often than index funds. Whenever you trade a stock, you create costs in the form of brokerage and potential tax consequences (tax on any profit you have made). Whereas most index funds rebalance (trade) only one to two times per year. Index funds tend to buy, hold and not trade – which is more effective in terms of costs.

The consequence of a lower trading environment is that with Australian index funds you can expect 40 to 50 per cent of the total return in income (and the rest in capital growth). Actively managed funds, on the other hand, tend to deliver 70 per cent or more of the overall return as income – being dividends plus realised capital gains each year. The higher the proportion of income you receive from your investments (including realised capital gain), the greater the tax consequences could be – and that needs to be considered as part of your overall investment strategy.

More diversification

You can invest in one index product and get exposure to 3000 or more different stocks. One of the benefits that comes from novice investors adopting a passive investment strategy is that it forces them to invest in a well-diversified manner. This is far superior to the average investor who invests in direct stocks – as typically most investors hold fewer than 20 stocks. Diversification is an important tenet of passive investing because the underlying thesis of the passive methodology is that no-one can pick a winner. Therefore, the lower risk way to invest is to hold a little bit of everything.

Understanding the insidious impact of high fees

The compounding impact of a small difference in fees can have a huge impact. Let me explain using an example. Let's imagine three friends, all aged 35 and all with $100,000 to invest in super. The three invest their money into three different super funds but are lucky enough to all benefit from the same gross investment return of 7 per cent p.a. They each contribute $9000 per year. At 60, they get together to compare their super balances. Here are their results:

- David invested in a retail fund (like Colonial, BT or AMP) and paid 2.0 per cent p.a. in fees. His balance was $735,000.

- Mark invested in an industry super fund and paid 0.60 per cent p.a. in investment fees plus $1.50 per week in admin fees. His super balance was $900,000.

- Sophie invested in a passive (index) investment option and paid weighted average investment fees of just 0.20 per cent p.a. Her balance was $950,000.

Like many people, they didn't realise how fees can have such a big financial impact. They each started with the same investment amount, made the same super contributions and achieved the same investment returns – and Sophie ended up with nearly 30 per cent more in retirement savings than David! Half a percentage point here and there doesn't sound like much, but fees add up (compound) – and that's why you need to be super-focused on them.

Comparing (chasing) returns becomes unimportant

When selecting which fund manager or superannuation fund to use, most people are very tempted to compare investment performance and returns. While this sounds like a logical thing to do, it often leads to the wrong conclusions.

Selecting a fund manager or super fund based on a comparison of historical investment returns alone is like following a tip from a friend who backed the winner of the Melbourne Cup last year. Just because your friend picked the winner last year doesn't necessarily mean she has a higher chance of picking the winner this year, does it?

Before we compare investment returns, we need to compare investment methodologies. Because, if we believe that an active investing methodology is highly likely to generate inferior returns, we need to discount any investment providers (including super funds) that use said investment strategy.

Comparing a super fund that uses an active investment methodology to a super fund that uses a passive investment methodology provides you with very little evidence of performance because the sample size is only two. In this situation, the active super fund may have outperformed the passive super fund in the past. However, as a very large body of research demonstrates (and as I have discussed in this chapter), whether the active super fund can continue to outperform the index consistently over the long term is highly uncertain. As such, before you go comparing (chasing) returns and performance, you must ensure you're comparing apples with apples (that is, the same investment methodologies are used).

Another important factor to note is that research has demonstrated that most investors who chase returns are late to the party. An active fund manager will receive a lot of new inflows (new investors investing with them) after a few stellar years. As we now know, outperforming the market year after year is very difficult. Research has demonstrated that most of these investors will have missed the boat – that is, the active fund manager notches up one or two years of great returns, people then invest in that fund manager and then in subsequent years they fail to beat the market. Research by Vanguard[1] has shown that investors who chase investment performance end up achieving an inferior long-term return by 2 to 3 per cent p.a. (the study was conducted over a 10-year period). To put that in context, the difference in today's dollars of a 5 per cent p.a. versus an 8 per cent p.a. investment return on $200,000 after 20 years is over $148,000 (meaning your investment balance ends up being over 45 per cent more).

In summary ... why passive is better than active

Let's take a moment now to summarise what we have covered so far:

- Far less than 50 per cent of active managers beat the market in any one year. In 2016, 33 per cent failed in Australia and 18 per cent in US. These failure rates usually range between 10 and 30 per cent. Therefore, picking a 'winning' active fund manager is a low probability sport.

- If you are lucky enough to pick an active fund manager that beats the market over the next 12 months, research tells us that outperformance rarely persists. Of the active fund managers that performed in the top quartile in 2012, only 1.3 per cent of those managers remained in the top quartile in 2016!

- The fees charged by active fund managers are between 3 and 20 times higher than passive managers – so you need not only to beat the market, but also beat it by a big margin to offset fees plus compensate you for the risk (that is, the risk that the manager will underperform).

Therefore, if you are going to invest using active fund managers you must:

- pick a fund manager that will beat the index – but odds are heavily stacked against you

- switch managers every one to three years because any outperformance nearly never persists

- do this so well (consistently) you earn enough to offset the higher fees, tax, transaction costs and risk.

Recommendation: don't bother. Invest in an index fund! And here are three reasons why this share investing approach works:

1. *Fees are low*: Typically, fees are less than 0.50 per cent p.a. – and this is important, because you keep more of the

investment returns. Therefore, you're under less pressure to consistently produce higher returns to offset higher fees.

2. *A rules-based approach is repeatable and testable*: An evidence-based approach means you can back-test – that is, you can apply the rules to work out what historical returns you would have produced if you invested applying these same rules. This approach doesn't rely on subjective assessments, in-house geniuses or talent. It's based on quantities and rules that can be applied without emotion and at a low cost. You don't have to put your 'faith' in a financial planner or fund manager coming up with a new idea every time.

3. *You don't even have to put your faith in one methodology*: Instead, you can employ various tested and proven methodologies – in other words, diversify. Different index methodologies will behave differently in different markets. Be incredibly meticulous about which methodologies you use – don't invest in anything without due diligence.

In the following sections, I take you through some of the methodologies available and how you can diversify within them.

Three passive/index methodologies

The definition of passive investing is the process of adopting a rules-based and evidence-based methodology to invest in an asset class. A rules-based approach means you don't have to rely on subjective decision-making, such as picking which stocks to invest in. The benefit of an evidence-based approach is that it is often rooted in academia, which allows it to be studied and critiqued. In addition, we can back-test these approaches to work out how they would have performed historically if we had adopted them decades ago.

Passive methodologies for index investment can be broken into three categories – some more effective than others. These three options are covered in the following sections.

Traditional market cap indexing

Traditional market capitalisation ('cap' for short) indexing works by allocating investment dollars based on the value of each company included in the index compared to the value of the index overall. For example, at the time of writing, Commonwealth Bank's market capitalisation was approximately $139 billion. The value of the top 200 companies in Australia is circa $1.72 trillion. Therefore, CBA's market cap represents 8.1 per cent of the S&P/ASX 200 index. So, if you invested in a traditional market cap S&P/ASX 200 index fund (for example, 'iShares Core S&P/ASX 200'), 8.1 per cent of your monies would be invested in CBA. The market cap fund invests in all the top 200 companies by their market cap proportion. Vanguard is the largest traditional market cap index provider in the world. (See later in this chapter for some of the criticisms levelled at this style of passive investing.)

Value investing passive funds

Passive funds that adopt a fundamental or value investing approach – sometimes referred to as 'smart beta' funds – use statistical methods other than price (that is, using share price to determine market cap) to allocate monies towards each company that makes up any given index. They still adopt a rules-based approach – meaning they're not using subjective decisions to work out how to invest in the top 200 companies, for example. Various methodologies are possible, but I like two value-based index methodologies the best:

1. *Fundamental indexing:* This was developed by Research Affiliates, Robert Arnott's firm, and focuses on allocating

investments based on economic value rather than market cap. The approach measures economic value for all index stocks using four company characteristics equally: sales, profit, dividends and book value (net assets). The investments are reweighted annually to take into account any changes in economic value. BetaShares, the Australian-based fund manager licensed to use this indexing approach, offers two products: one that invests in the top 200 Australian companies and another that invests in the top 1000 US companies. BetaShares has back-tested this strategy in the Australian market over the 10 years ending in March 2017 and has shown this approach has beaten traditional indexing by 2.47 per cent p.a. (and by 2.3 per cent p.a. over 20 years).

2. *Dimensional investing:* Fund manager Dimensional Fund Advisors uses this value methodology exclusively. Based on academic research, they believe that certain dimensions of a stock are responsible for producing higher expected returns. Therefore, a portfolio should be tilted towards these different dimensions. Dimensional Fund Advisors focuses on three dimensions: company size (smaller companies produce better returns), relative price (value stocks are those with lower price-to-book ratios) and profitability (highly profitable companies tend to generate better returns). The fund manager applies a number of investment rules to filter out stocks contained in an index that it doesn't want to invest in because these stocks don't provide exposure to one of these dimensions. Because it uses a rules-based approach, its fees are low, and they are not considered to be an active manager. This approach has very strong roots in academia, with several Nobel Laureates acting as consults and/or independent directors.

Typically, you can only access Dimensional Fund investing via an independent financial advisor. (They include these restrictions to be unattractive to short-term and erratic investors, reducing turnover within the portfolio. This means they are selective about what advisors they deal with.) However, I understand that Dimensional Fund Advisors are launching a public direct option in 2018 – so watch this space.

As the passive investment management industry grows and matures further, I expect more non-price related strategies to emerge so ensure you keep up to date – go to my website (www.investopoly.com.au) to sign up to my blog, which will keep you informed of the latest news.

Equal weight indexing

Equal weight indexing allocates investments towards companies on an equal weight basis. For example, if you invested $200 in a top 200 equal weight index fund, $1 of your monies would be invested in each of the top 200 companies.

This methodology is very basic and lacks common sense and, therefore, is not widely used. I have never recommended this methodology.

Criticisms of traditional market cap index investing

A few criticisms have been levied at traditional market cap indexing, which I discuss here.

Index arbitrage

Companies such as S&P and Dow Jones are responsible for managing certain indexes, and these indexes are reweighted every so often – typically every six months. At this time, companies are either added or subtracted from a given index (and reweighted). This creates demand for these stocks.

Market participants know that index funds must either buy or sell said stocks on the day that they are added or subtracted from an index – so their holdings are still aligned with the index. As such, studies have shown that the price of the stock that is being added to an index typically appreciates between 5 and 10 per cent when its reweighting is announced. However, the stock loses most of those gains within approximately two weeks after being added to the index. This means that traditional market cap index funds tend to buy stocks at inflated prices. The same is true when a stock is removed from the index – in that the market price becomes temporarily depressed so the index fund must sell when the price is low. Studies estimate[1] that the trading cost of such events amounts to approximately 0.28 per cent for traditional index funds.

Follows price bubbles

Another criticism of traditional market cap indexing is that, as the price of a stock increases, an index fund needs to hold more of said stock. If a price bubble occurs (stock becomes overvalued), this traditional market cap indexing approach increases your exposure to it. For example, between 1987 and 2000, the valuation of tech stocks was appreciating at an alarming rate. However, the NASDAQ index fell by nearly 80 per cent between the year 2000 and 2002 due to the dot-com bubble bursting. Some index funds (depending on the index they tracked) would have had to track this level of exposure. As such, many people believe price is not always a reliable indicator of long-term value.

While traditional market cap indexing has its flaws, the undeniable truth is that it has still beaten the clear majority of active funds over the long run.

Diversify methodologies

While I think the criticisms of market cap indexing outlined in the preceding sections are valid, I note that in a recent interview Burton Malkiel (author of *A Random Walk Down Wall Street*) acknowledged that 'while traditional market cap indexing has its pitfalls, the undeniable truth is that despite this, it has still beaten the vast majority of active funds'.

I think the best solution is to diversify among index methodologies – that is, use a combination of traditional market and value indexing. In some markets, for example, when markets are at their peak, you might tilt your portfolio to be overweight in value indexing and underweight in traditional market cap indexing – to mitigate the impact of price bubbles. I believe this is very important.

Be careful about adopting any old methodology

Many different index methodologies and products are available on the market, so you need to thoroughly research these before investing. You need to ascertain whether what you are investing in will actually work (that is, it's based on sound fundamentals) or if it's just 'slick marketing' that's making it look attractive. Use the information already provided in this chapter to help with this analysis.

Ways to invest in passive funds

Once you've made the decision to invest in passive index funds, you have two main ways to do so, covered in the following sections.

Managed funds

As an investor, you can buy units in an index managed fund, thereby gaining exposure to said index investment. Most managed funds have a minimum investment of $5000, and you can make a managed fund investment by contacting the provider directly and completing the application form. Most fund managers provide online access so that you can track the performance of your investment. The largest provider of index managed funds is Vanguard.

Exchange traded funds

Exchange traded funds (ETFs) are essentially the same as managed funds except that they're listed on the ASX. Most, but not all, ETFs tend to be passively managed index funds. To invest in said funds all you must do is buy shares in them using an online trading account or share broker. As such, no minimum investment exists. As discussed already in this chapter, ETFs are becoming increasingly popular in Australia and around the world – at the time of writing, 133 ETFs are listed in Australia (you can find the current list on the ASX website – www.asx.com.au). Their investment management fees typically range from 0.05 to 0.80 per cent p.a. The main Australian ETF providers include:

- BetaShares

- iShares (owned by Blackrock)

- SPDR (pronounced spider; owned by State Street Global Advisors)

- VanEck
- Vanguard.

A case study: constructing a portfolio

Let's pull all the information provided so far in this chapter together using a case study. Ian and Karen are in their thirties and have $50,000 of cash savings that they would like to invest in shares. They would also like to make additional investments of $1,500 per month into this portfolio. Given the relatively low value of their investment, I suggest that they use ETFs (purchased via a low-cost online share trading platform such as provided by CMC Markets). Ian and Karen then need to go through three steps to construct a portfolio, covered in the following sections.

Decide on an asset allocation

As we discussed in Golden Rule #5, you need to work out what asset allocation is appropriate for your circumstances. Given Ian and Karen's age and the relative value of their initial investment, I suggest investing it with an 80/20 asset allocation (that is, 80 per cent in growth assets and 20 per cent in defensive assets). In respect to the 80 per cent in growth assets, I suggest that they invest 45 per cent in the Australian market and 35 per cent in the international market (slightly more Aussie for the higher dividends and imputation credits).

Decide on the passive investing methodologies

To diversify methodology risk, I then suggest using an equal combination of traditional market cap indexing and value indexing. Using Dimensional Fund investing would also be good, but to access these investments we would have to use an investment platform, which would give rise to additional costs and this is not worthwhile for the size of Ian and Karen's investments (but if your have more money to invest, speak to an independent financial advisor).

Select the ETFs

A list of available ETFs can be found on the ASX's website (www. asx.com.au – they call them Exchange Traded Products or ETPs). The following table lists the ETFs I suggest Ian and Karen invest in, along with their fees and the percentage allocation suggested.

Stock code	Name	Asset class and investment style	Fees	Allocation
BOND	SPDR S&P/ASX Australian Bond Fund	Australian bonds	0.24%	10.0%
IHHY	iShares Global High Yield Bond (AUD Hedged)	International bonds	0.56%	10.0%
QOZ	BetaShares FTSE RAFI Australia 200	Fundamental indexing into top 200 Australian shares	0.40%	22.5%
VAS	Vanguard Australian Shares Index	Traditional market cap indexing in the top Australian 300 shares	0.14%	22.5%

Stock code	Name	Asset class and investment style	Fees	Allocation
QUS	BetaShares FTSE RAFI U.S. 1000	Fundamental indexing into the top 1000 US shares	0.40%	17.5%
VGS	Vanguard MSCI Index International Shares	Traditional market cap indexing in the top global 1600 shares (ex-Aust.)	0.18%	17.5%
Total weighted average investment costs			0.30%	100%

Important warning: check for updates

This is an example portfolio only and, of course, it will not necessarily be appropriate for all readers' circumstances. I have included the case study here to demonstrate the steps in constructing a simple portfolio. That said, I will update this when required (to account for new products, changes and so on) so before you proceed with constructing your own portfolio, please check if I have made any updates at www.investopoly.com.au.

If you have more than $100,000 to invest, get some advice

While implementing a passive investment approach can be a relatively simple thing to do, mistakes can easily be made. Therefore, if you have no interest in share investing and/or if you have more than $100,000 to invest, I believe you should engage the services of an independent advisor to help you (but read the final chapter before you do that). This will ensure that you don't make any mistakes and you can leverage the advisor's experience and expertise in making tilts and adjustments.

Having an advisor look after a portfolio of passively invested assets (valued at less than $1 million) should cost somewhere in the range of $1,000 to $3,000 p.a. Therefore, over the long term (say, 20 years), the advisor only must save or make you an average of 0.10 per cent p.a. extra to more than offset their fees. If they do this, their service is essentially free. Engaging someone with decades of experience who also continues to educate themselves (to a level that you probably don't have the time to replicate) must be worth way more than 0.10 per cent p.a.! Remember, the more money you have invested, the more you have to lose (and potentially gain).

How to apply what you have learnt to your super

You can also use the information outlined in this chapter to maximise your superannuation. Firstly, let's look at the six basic types of super funds you can choose from:

1. *Retail funds:* These funds are often sold by financial advisors, with the fund providers typically owned by the big banks and operated to make a profit. The largest retail fund providers are AMP, Colonial (owned by CBA), BT (Westpac), MLC (NAB) and OnePath (ANZ). On average, retail funds tend to charge fees in the range of 1.30 to 1.90 per cent p.a. (or more) depending on your investments.

2. *Industry funds:* These funds are operated as not-for-profit entities (you may have seen them advertised on the TV). The larger industry funds include AustralianSuper, UniSuper, REST, Sunsuper, HESTA and CBus. Industry super funds typically charge fees in the range of 0.60 to 0.80 per cent p.a.

3. *Self-managed super funds:* This is the fastest growing sector of the market – although not really for any good reason in

my opinion. Fees to run an SMSF can range from $1,000 to $5,000 p.a., depending on the size and complexity of the investments.

4. *Employer funds:* Your employer may run its own fund – the largest being Telstra Super Scheme. Fees for these funds tend to be somewhere in the middle of those charged by retail and industry super funds, depending on the fund's size, typically in the range of 0.80 to 1.20 per cent p.a. Most people can elect to not use the employer's super fund but there may be benefits in doing so (such as free insurance).

5. *Public sector funds:* If you work for the government, you might be able to join a public fund such as the Commonwealth Superannuation Scheme, Public Sector Superannuation Scheme, QSuper or First State Super. Fees charged by public sector funds are typically in the range of 0.60 to 0.70 per cent p.a.

6. *Investment platform (wraps):* This is a simpler alternative to having an SMSF. A platform will typically allow you to invest in all listed shares (including ETFs) and managed funds. The only thing you cannot do with a platform is invest in direct property (you'll need an SMSF to do this). BT Wrap and Asgard are the two biggest players in Australia, although my preference is to use Macquarie Wrap.

Which super options to use

Of the six listed in the preceding section, the only options that can offer a totally passive approach include a few industry funds, an SMSF or a wrap platform.

If you have less than $200,000 in super, the best solution is an industry fund, and AustralianSuper, Sunsuper and Hostplus all offer pre-mixed 100 per cent indexed (passive) options. However, these are pretty basic and only use traditional market cap indexing.

Another option is to use AustralianSuper's Member Direct option, which allows you to construct your own ETF portfolio. The fee for this option is $395 p.a. so it's quite low cost but is a hands-on solution (which is not suitable for everyone).

If you have more than $200,000 in super, I would caution you in trying to do it yourself. A good independent financial advisor should more than pay for their fees in added value (returns). And it shouldn't cost that much (as noted earlier in this chapter). They can use a wrap platform and ensure you have exposure to all passive investing methodologies where appropriate (including reviewing new methodologies as they arise). Furthermore, super is a complex and dynamic environment (the rules are always changing) so if you have a substantial amount invested, you need someone on your team to look after you.

Three ways to maximise your super

When considering investment options for your super, keep in mind you need to do three things to maximise your super balance:

1. Minimise fees

2. Maximise investment returns

3. Contribute as much as possible as soon as possible.

Investing passively (as discussed throughout this chapter) will help you achieve the first two items. The following section looks at the impact of increased contributions.

What impact do additional super contributions have?

To give you a better idea of how much of an impact additional super contributions can have, let's look at another case study. Susie is 30 years old and earning a salary of $100,000 a year – so she is already contributing $9,500 per annum into super (via her employer's contributions). If Susie contributed an extra 3.5 per cent p.a. of her gross salary (that is, $3,500 p.a. or $67 per week), by age 60, her super balance would be 32 per cent higher ($965,000 versus $1.27 million). That is a big reward for a relatively small sacrifice.

Compare this to someone who starts a lot later in life. Matt is 50 years old and his super balance is $400,000. Matt's salary is $150,000 p.a. so his employer is contributing $14,250 p.a. into super. Even if Matt makes additional contributions so that his total contributions equal the concessional contribution cap (that is, the maximum you can contribute – $25,000 per annum at the time of writing), by age 60, Matt's super balance will only be 13 per cent higher ($845,000 versus $955,000). I think you'll agree that's a relatively small reward for a significant amount of additional contributions (approximately $100,000 in additional contributions over 10 years).

These two examples demonstrate that making additional contributions is a relatively ineffective investment strategy unless you begin making them when you're in your thirties. That is not to say that you shouldn't make them if you are older than this, however, because doing so is a good 'force-savings plan'.

The importance of rebalancing your portfolio

One final point to remember is that you need to keep in mind how your share and super investments fit in with your overall investment portfolio, regularly rebalancing your portfolio to ensure your balance is invested according to the asset allocation you have predetermined as appropriate for your circumstances. Rebalancing helps smooth returns (through reducing volatility) and, ultimately, maximise your return.

For example, if the share market has had a 'good' year and risen, say, 40 per cent, it is important that you reduce your allocation in this asset. This essentially forces you to take profit and reinvest some money in other asset classes (that have not performed as well). Put differently, rebalancing makes you move money from asset classes that are arguably overvalued into asset classes that might be undervalued. Research suggests that most stock market runs last, on average, approximately nine months. Therefore, you should not rebalance more often than that (so you can capture most of the returns). In fact, I recommend rebalancing annually.

The following table sets out the results of $100,000 invested in 1993 until the end of 2016, and demonstrates the difference between rebalancing and not.

	Rebalanced annually	Not rebalanced
Starting balance (1 Jan 1993)	$100,000	$100,000
Ending balance (31 Dec 2016)	$757,000	$716,000
Compound annual growth rate	8.80%	8.55%

You will note that the investor who rebalanced annually generated a higher return by 0.25 per cent p.a.

Golden Rule #6 summary

Throughout this chapter we have discussed:

- When investing in the share market, investors tend to make one (or all) of four mistakes: not adopting a proven methodology (investing in an ad hoc manner), being driven by fear or greed (trying to produce quick profit), not having enough patience (jumping from one investment to the next), and having little to no diversification (all their eggs in a couple of baskets).

- Two basic investing methodologies are available: active and passive management.

- A large body of research indicates that the vast majority of active funds fail to beat the index. Therefore, when trying to 'pick' an active manager, the odds are stacked against you. Only a small number of managers will beat the index in the next five years and a completely different set of managers will beat the index in the following five years – outperformance rarely persists. Therefore, passive management is a superior strategy.

- Other benefits of passive management include fees are typically 3 to 10 times lower, investment turnover is reduced, which means lower costs and tax, and diversification is higher.

- The fees you pay are very important. With fees, you don't get what you pay for – the lower the fees, the more money you retain.

- The three main index methodologies I recommend using are traditional market cap indexing and two non-price related methodologies (fundamental indexing and dimensional). Diversifying methodologies addresses the two main criticisms of traditional market cap indexing (index arbitrage and following price bubbles).

- You can access index funds via managed investment (direct with the provider) and/or exchange traded funds.

- You can use ETFs (available via the ASX) to construct your passive portfolio.

- You can apply the same passive investing principles to maximise your super.

- Regularly rebalancing your overall portfolio to ensure you maintain your predetermined asset allocation is important. I recommend rebalancing annually.

1 'Quantifying the Impact of Chasing Fund Performance', Vanguard Research, July 2014.

2 See, for example, 'Cost and Capacity: Comparing Smart Beta Strategies', by Tzee Chow, Feifei Li, Alex Pickard and Yadwinder Garg, www.researchaffiliates.com, July 2017.

GOLDEN RULE #7

ONLY INVEST IN 'INVESTMENT-GRADE' PROPERTY

Successfully investing in property is relatively simple. Too often, however, simple mistakes are made – and investing in the wrong property is the biggest mistake by far. The wrong asset will never produce adequate investment returns. What you need is a good understanding of the three attributes that a property must possess to be deemed investment-grade.

Throughout this chapter I share with you a robust, evidence-based and easy-to-understand methodology for investing in property. I explain the three attributes that must be present and what I mean by 'investment-grade' property. Property investment, if implemented correctly, can help you accumulate substantial wealth – but first, let's look at some of the common mistakes property investors make.

Some simple reasons most property investors fail

Over the past 15 years I've met literally thousands of property investors. From these, I estimate that 80 per cent of property investors fail to generate adequate investment returns. As such, these property investors would actually be better off investing in something else. In my opinion, if you're going to invest, you do it properly or you don't do it at all.

The biggest and most common mistake that property investors make is investing in property that doesn't have the fundamentals to drive perpetual capital growth. Asset selection (selecting the correct property) is responsible for 80 per cent or more of your investment returns. If you get the asset selection right and everything else wrong, chances are you will still do very well out of investing in property. Therefore, if you're going to invest in property, my advice to you is to be obsessive about nailing the asset selection. I can't stress this enough.

The property industry is opaque at times

Buyer beware! While a lot of ethical and professional people are in the property industry, some people, like in most industries, are only concerned about lining their own pockets. The property industry can, at times, be full of conflicts of interest and opaque marketing tactics – things such as paying referral fees, kickbacks, commissions and spotter fees. You may even be offered a rebate off the sale price listed on the contract of sale, so to third parties it looks like the property sold for a higher price than it actually did – and the list goes on. I don't want to paint an overly negative picture of the property industry but I am trying to highlight to you to be very careful. If you don't have a lot of experience dealing with property, you might like to consider having someone you trust represent you. This could be a friend, family member or buyers' agent (I talk more about buyers' agents later in this chapter).

When talking about 'property', be specific

When we talk about 'property', what are we talking about? Are we talking about all houses? Are we talking about all properties in Toorak (in Melbourne)? If we're not specific, our conversation becomes meaningless! You see, most commentators (that is, those in the media) talk about property as if it's a homogenous asset class – and that couldn't be further from the truth. The Australian property market is made up of thousands of different smaller markets. For example, the Melbourne property market is very different to Darwin's. A suburb on the eastern side of Melbourne is very different to a suburb on the western side of Melbourne. Even different streets in the same suburb will perform differently. Therefore, when we talk about 'property', we really need to define what we are talking about. For the purposes of this book, when I refer to property I'm talking specifically about investment-grade property.

If you watch and listen to the media, what you find is that most of the commentary about the property market doesn't apply to investment-grade property (or if it does, it applies to a much lesser extent). So, when you see a headline that property prices are about to crash, you need to ask yourself whether they're really suggesting that all property will fall in value. When the journalist lists the assumptions behind their prediction of a property crash, you will often find that investment-grade property will largely be immune to many of these factors. I'm not suggesting that invest-ment-grade property is bullet-proof (and has no risk). However, what I am suggesting is that you need to be very careful about the definition of 'property'.

What is investment-grade property?

I define investment-grade property as any property that has the fundamentals and historical track record of appreciating in value by between 4 and 5 per cent per annum above inflation over the long term. According to the RBA, inflation has averaged 2.5 per cent p.a. over the past 20 years. Therefore, investment-grade property has a nominal growth rate of 6.5 to 7.5 per cent or above.

Put simply, investment-grade property should double in value every 7 to 12 years. I appreciate this is a wide range but different grades of investment-grade property are possible, and different inflationary environments will influence returns.

Investment-grade bonds are normally classified into four categories: AAA, AA, A and BBB. AAA bonds are the highest rated bonds (that is, the highest quality and the lowest risk). Any bond rated lower than BBB is not considered to be investment-grade.

In the same way, I suggest that investment-grade property also has sub-categories as illustrated by the table below.

Rating	Expected return (p.a.)	Example property
AAA	8.5% to 12% or more	2-bedroom, single-fronted Victorian cottage in prime suburb on a quiet street in Hawthorn, Melbourne
AA to A	7.5% to 10%	2-bedroom, art-deco apartment in a block of only 6 other apartments in a quiet street in Bondi, Sydney
BBB	6% to 9%	1-bedroom, 1960s–1970s apartment in a block of 10 in Richmond, Melbourne

Admittedly, the grades and examples used in the preceding table are subjective. However, the purpose of this table is to help you understand that not all investment-grade properties can be considered equal. That is, an AAA-rated property will probably double in value between 7 and 10 years, whereas a BBB-rated property will take a bit longer to double in value – probably in the range of 10 to 12 years. In short, an AAA-rated property will often provide more capital growth and be considered a lower risk investment.

Asset selection: Choosing the 'right' property

I believe three attributes are common to all investment-grade properties. Therefore, if you want to select investment-grade assets, you need to simply make sure they possess these three attributes. Having two out of three is not good enough – you must have all three! The following sections run through these three attributes, and why they are so important.

Attribute 1: Correct proportion of land value

A property's value is the aggregate of two components – the value of the building plus the value of the land. Over time, land appreciates whereas buildings depreciate (go down in value). The goal with property is that the amount of appreciation in the land component more than offsets the building depreciation over the long run – thereby the total value of the asset appreciates.

Let me explain using an example. Consider two properties worth $1 million each. The first property has a land value of $800,000 and a building value of $200,000. The second property has a land value of $300,000 and a building value of $700,000. Assuming buildings depreciate at a rate of 2.5 per cent p.a., let's calculate how much the land needs to appreciate for these properties to be worth $2 million each in 10 years' time:

- The building value of the first property will depreciate to $156,000 in 10 years' time. Therefore, the land value component needs to appreciate from $800,000 to $1.85 million – which requires an average compound growth rate of 8.7 per cent p.a.

- The second property's building value will have depreciated to $547,000 in 10 years' time, so its land value needs to appreciate from $300,000 to $1.45 million – or an average compounding rate of 17 per cent. This is approximately double the growth rate of the first property!

Which property would you feel comfortable investing in?

A property needs to have a substantial land value component for it to be able to achieve an adequate rate of capital growth. Put differently, it is impossible for a property to appreciate in value over the long run if it does not have a strong land value component.

A common misconception is that apartments don't have any land value. This is not true – apartments have an attributable land value component. For example, consider a block of six apartments that sit on a very valuable parcel of land – for example, 800 m² in Hawthorn, Victoria. If the land value was $3 million, then, notionally, each apartment has an attributable land value of $500,000 (being one-sixth of the total value). The problem with high-rise apartments is that, while they typically sit on very valuable parcels of land, there might be 200 or more apartments, so their attributable land value component is very small. For example, if the land value is $10 million, the attributable land value component is only $50,000 (being $10 million divided by 200).

Attribute 1 rule: The proportion of land value must be greater than 50 per cent for apartments and over 60 per cent for houses for a property to be considered investment-grade.

Attribute 2: Scarcity

The laws of supply and demand are easy to understand. If demand exceeds supply, you will see perpetual upward pressure on prices – because the sale goes to the person who is prepared to pay the most. Ideally, you want to enter a market with 10 potential buyers for every one seller.

Two components typically drive a property's scarcity: location and architectural style.

Location of the land

For the location of the land to influence scarcity, two things must be present:

1. Land must be located in a highly desirable location

2. The land supply in that location must be scarce.

As discussed in the preceding attribute, you need a strong land value component – but not just any land will do. You only want scarce land, and several factors make the land scarce. Firstly, supply needs to be fixed. That is, you should invest in a location with no vacant land available (at least not within 10 kilometres or more). This is why new-build estates rarely make good investments – because an abundant supply of land is usually available in the surrounding area.

Secondly, the land should be located close to as many amenities as possible to ensure it's in high demand (but short supply). Some examples of amenities that make a location desirable include:

- *Shopping options*: A 'village' feel or shopping strip is best because this creates a community feel/vibe.

- *Health facilities*: These should include doctors, dentists and hospitals.

135

- *Recreational areas:* Parks, running tracks, movies, cafes, restaurants and entertainment venues all make a location attractive.

- *Education facilities:* The property should be close to schools, particularly ones with good reputations and/or good private schools.

- *Transport options:* Property that is close to public transport and easily accessible by road (that is, close to major arterial roads) will be in high demand.

- *Quiet enjoyment:* The land/property should be located on a quiet street away from traffic, commercial businesses and other noise and eyesores.

Architectural style and orientation of the property

A property's architectural style can also add to a property's scarcity. Some architectural styles are timeless and have wide appeal – the Victorian style is a good example. Some styles, on the other hand, have dated badly – 1980s-style properties, for instance, tend to look pretty unattractive these days. Using the Victorian style as an example, the supply of this style is reducing – very few new properties are being built in a Victorian style (pretty much none) and some of the old ones that are in disrepair are being demolished. However, they do have wide appeal – so demand is increasing while supply is decreasing. This imbalance in demand and supply puts upwards pressure on price and value.

The architectural style of a property must be in keeping with the area. For example, in some suburbs and locations, weatherboard Victorian cottages are very common. However, in other areas, double-brick Federation homes are more common and a weatherboard cottage might look out of place (and so less attractive to buyers). It wouldn't make sense to invest in a property that is not in keeping with its surrounds.

Finally, the orientation of the block and property, the level of natural light, privacy provided and a logical floor plan all add to the scarcity (demand) of the property. A property having good natural light and adequate privacy (that is, a view unimpaired by ugly industrial property or affected by noise pollution) is seen positively. A logical floor plan means toilets should be as far away from the living and eating areas as possible, rooms should be large enough to be practical and so on.

One key point to remember is the difference between *scarcity* and *anomalous*. Scarce assets are highly desirable by a broad section of the population. Anomalous assets appeal to a mere few. An example of an anomalous property is one that has been painted in fluorescent pink. Not many fluorescent pink properties are around so they are scarce, but they are not very desirable. Proprieties that are abnormal or not in keeping with their surrounds rarely make good investments.

In summary, the best way to explain scarcity is to draw an analogy with diamonds. When selecting a property, we don't want a diamond, we want a pink diamond. Pink is one of the scarcest colours of all diamonds and as such is worth more than 11 times a normal white diamond. A pink diamond is scarce, not anomalous.

Attribute 2 rule: You must invest in a property that has ten or more potential purchasers for every one seller (that is, demand is far greater than supply).

Attribute 3: Proven performance

Successful investing is not about speculating with your money – it is about earning the highest return for the lowest risk. Risk is defined as the probability that investment returns will deviate from what is expected. Say you're considering two investment properties. Option one has a 30 per cent chance of generating a 16 per cent p.a. growth rate. Option two has a 95 per cent chance of achieving an 8 per cent p.a. growth rate. Which option would you prefer? Option two is the clear winner in my opinion.

If you invest in a property with an average growth rate of 8 per cent p.a., in 30 years the property will be worth 10 times its current value. You only need to invest in a couple of properties like that to be independently wealthy. Therefore, at this point, your focus isn't on maximising returns, it's minimising risk – that is, investing in a property that is as close to a 'sure thing' as possible.

One of the best ways you can reduce your risk when investing in a property is to study its past performance – and the performance of comparable properties located in very close proximity.

Is past performance a reliable indicator of future performance? For property, yes, it is. The reason I say that is because the value-drivers for property – that is, land value and scarcity, as discussed in attributes 1 and 2 – tend to be static and factual. These attributes rarely change – or, if they do, they take many decades to change. For example, things like land size and orientation don't change, and neither does proximity to schools and hospitals – schools and hospitals rarely relocate – and so on. These value-drivers are also a question of fact – they are objective rather than subjective. They either exist or they do not. Therefore, the hypothesis is if these value-drivers have been responsible for the level of capital growth in the past, and no evidence exists that this will change in the future, then we can broadly expect the same comparable performance in the future. So if a property has appreciated in value by 8 per cent p.a. over the last 30 years – whereas median property value has appreciated by, say, 6 per cent p.a. over the same period – I would conclude that it is very likely that this property will perform better than the median over the long term.

I am very surprised by the number of people who invest in a property without any regard to its past growth. If a property has only grown in value by 3 per cent p.a. over the past 30 years, why take the risk on investing in it now? The future growth might be better than its historical growth, sure, but why take the risk? Why not invest in a sure thing – a property that has appreciated in value by 11 per cent p.a. over the past 30 years, for example? I'm not saying you'll get 11 per cent p.a. over the next 30 years. All I'm suggesting is that if it has grown at this rate in the past, the property must have some positive fundamental attributes. And it is these attributes that will probably drive (or at least influence) future growth. Again, no-one has any idea of what future growth will be – but all we need to do is pick assets that are 'pink diamonds' and we will be well positioned to capture any returns that might be available.

Attribute 3 rule: Only invest in a property that has proven its ability to appreciate in value over the long term.

Warning: Off-the-plan and new-build property make bad investments

Off-the-plan (buying a property before it's been constructed) and new-build properties (such as townhouses) almost never make good investments because they compromise all three of the preceding attributes:

- Their land value proportion is typically less than 10 per cent, and often closer to 5 per cent or even less. This means you are paying mostly for building value, and buildings depreciate in value. (Low land value compromises attribute 1.)

- These properties are often located in large complexes with many other properties that look identical. In addition, they are located in an impaired location (for example, on a main road). This means supply is often larger than demand. (Low scarcity compromises attribute 2.)

- Because these properties have not been bought and sold previously, they have not proven their ability to generate capital growth. In addition, ascertaining their market value is very difficult. The sale price is the aggregate of three components: the site cost + construction cost + the developer's profit margin. This amount may or may not represent fair market value. (No proven performance compromises attribute 3.)

A further factor is that these properties are designed and built to optimise the first sale, without virtually any consideration to optimising resale. The developer is in it for the short term – which is at odds with the investor's requirements. So they tend to look old (suffer wear and tear) very quickly.

If you only learn one thing from reading this book, I hope it's the lesson to never, ever invest in an off-the-plan or new-build property. Please ignore all the slick marketing. Ignore the idea of a sparkling new property. Ignore the stamp duty savings, depreciation benefits, rental incentives, and so on. Only focus on the fundamental factors that drive property value (or their lack thereof).

Pay for asset selection advice only if you find the *right* advisor

Warren Buffett says, 'Price is what you pay; value is what you get'. This quote could not be more appropriate for a discussion about professional investment property advisors (often called 'buyers' agents').

The trap when selecting an investment property is that once you understand the fundamentals (that is, the three required attributes discussed earlier), it all seems quite simple. This means many people think they can select an investment-grade property without any professional advice or even a second opinion. I don't want to overcomplicate the process. Property is a simple asset to understand at a high level. However, acquiring an adequate level of knowledge and experience in any one particular market location does take many years of experience. You see, you only have to be a little wrong to miss out on a lot of the investment returns. A property rated 8 out of 10 (quality wise) might only appreciate in value by, say, 5 per cent p.a. However, a 10 out of 10 property might produce a growth rate of, say, 8 per cent p.a. or more. In this regard, your asset selection must be perfect.

Let me put it a different way. The cost of making a mistake – selecting a dud asset or one that is less than perfect – is significant. Yes, it will cost you money (in terms of lost growth). A 2 per cent growth differential (say, 6 per cent p.a. versus 8 per cent p.a.) on a $750,000 property will cost you over $665,000 in today's dollars in terms of missed growth after 20 years (and more than twice that amount after 30 years). However, the costliest consequence of making a mistake is lost time – that is, the amount of time you waste holding onto an underperforming investment. You may be able to make up for lost money, but you will never make up for lost time. And as I discussed in Golden Rule #4, time is a necessary ingredient for any low-risk investment strategy.

As in any industry, you find good and not-so-good operators in the buyers' agent industry. Dealing with a trustworthy, professional, independent and reputable buyers' agent is critically important. The following are some of the hallmarks of a good buyers' agent:

- They can explain to you what factors drive value and why a particular property is investment-grade and why another isn't – and their answer shouldn't be 'fluff'. You are looking for a clear articulation of their reasoning. I have found that some buyers' agents really don't understand what makes a good investment property – they're merely trying to complete a transaction to generate a commission. These are not the buyers' agents you want to deal with. A good buyers' agent has a very strict investment methodology/philosophy that they adhere to.

Note that assessing property does use a combination of art and science. Therefore, sometimes certain properties in certain locations just won't work as investments and no objective reasons might exist for this – but these are exceptions rather than the rule. In the main, a good buyers' agent will be able to objectively explain why a property is a good investment or not.

- They don't listen to you. Yes, that's right. I believe a good buyers' agent will not listen to their client. Let me explain. I have seen some buyers' agents compromise investment fundamentals and principles just to buy a property for a client. However, a reputable buyers' agent will never compromise their professional advice just to please a client. A buyers' agent's job is to help their client make as much money as possible from investing in property. Sometimes clients need to be saved from themselves (in other words, not listened to). For any reputable professional, doing work they are proud of is more important that making money. Professionalism should never be compromised just to make a sale.

- They can show you examples of properties they have bought for clients in the last ten years (or more). This means you can measure the capital growth rate for these properties – and you want evidence of good growth. You should then ask to see examples of properties they have bought for clients in the past year. What you are looking for here is that the property types are relatively similar. This shows that they have a strict methodology and they are not simply marketing whatever property is popular to their clients at any one time. I have seen some disreputable buyers' agents chop and change the types of property they recommend to clients – which might be driven by their desire to maintain a certain volume of business. This demonstrates a complete absence of methodology (they don't stand for anything) and suggests they are more interested in generating commission than building wealth for their clients.

- They specialise in a particular market. I have seen some buyers' agents advertise that they can help clients in various markets – sometimes in different states and even countries! In practice, unless you have a large team of people, this is difficult to do. When you engage a buyers' agent, you're paying for an individual's knowledge and expertise in a specific market. You need them to be an expert in their area – they must have an intimate knowledge of the area you are buying in. For example, if I wanted to buy an investment property in Cremorne in Sydney, I would use a buyers' agent who specialises in the Lower North Shore.

- They have been in business for a long period of time. While a shorter time in business is not a deal-breaker per se, a longer length of experience does provide you with more confidence. Firstly, the fact that they have been in business for a long period of time will give you some evidence. If you Google their name you might be able to find reviews from past clients. Secondly, it means they have experience across various property cycles and markets, which is important.

- They have a real estate licence, professional indemnity insurance and so forth. These are basic requirements for all buyers' agents.

If any of the preceding items are not present in a buyers' agent you're considering working with, do not take the risk. Keep looking until you find someone you can trust.

In terms of fees, buyers' agents usually charge a percentage fee in the range of 2 to 3 per cent of a property's value. The level of fees that established and reputable buyers' agents charge does not vary that much – so don't choose based on price.

How many properties do you need?

How many properties do you think you need to own to generate sufficient wealth to fund a comfortable retirement? Most people have no idea. Some people think they need 5, 10 or more properties!

Of course, the answer will be different for everyone because it depends on your income, existing assets, time until you retire, goals and other factors. However, having been involved in developing hundreds of investment strategies (possibly more than a thousand), I can tell you that 95 per cent of people need to hold somewhere between one and three investment properties. It is unusual for an average person to need to invest in more than three properties.

Indeed, the number of properties is not really the most relevant measure. More important is the *quality* of the assets that you own and the amount of equity you have in them. I would prefer to own only one sensational investment property compared to three average ones.

Some books and property promoters suggest that investors should aim for acquiring more than three investment properties. However, I fail to see how this could work. You either have to acquire several low-value properties (and are therefore likely to compromise the asset quality, meaning they aren't investment-grade) or, if you are buying investment-grade property, you must borrow a significant amount of money. I have seen profiles of investors (in property magazines) who have $2 million to $3 million in loans when their family income is between $100,000 and $150,000 p.a. in total. This is a very high-risk approach and a recipe for disaster in my opinion.

Debt is a great servant but a very bad master. You must control it, not the other way around. Therefore, when borrowing to invest in property you must conservatively assess your capacity to be able to service the debt and sleep at night. Also, you need to have a debt exit strategy. That is, how will you repay the debt when you retire? I typically like my clients to have little to no debt when they enter retirement because, at this stage of life, they will be very sensitive to interest rate changes (because their only income source is investment income). Therefore, if an investment strategy involves borrowing a lot of money to invest, you must also develop a plan for how you will reduce debt before retirement. (I discuss your debt exit strategy in more detail towards the end of this chapter.)

Constructing your investment property portfolio

You need to consider a few factors when constructing or planning out what types of properties you will include in your property portfolio. These factors relate to diversification of your portfolio and include:

- *Diversifying geographically*: Spread your properties among different suburbs and market segments, and even consider investing in different capital cities. The idea behind this is that markets do not grow uniformly so, by diversifying geographically, you will hopefully smooth your return (growth). Growing your asset value will allow you to access further equity to assist you in building wealth. I realise that it is tempting to invest in one location you know well. However, the benefits of diversification should not be discounted. (See my comments on land tax in the next section for more on why you should look as far as different states for investment options.)

- *Diversifying across various price points*: Different sectors of the market (in terms of price points) will perform differently at different times – mainly because different buyers drive this performance. For example, if you have an investment apartment already, then you could look at buying a house for your next investment – and vice versa. Stick closely to the median value within a suburb too – because that is the price point likely to attract the largest volume of buyers.

- *Diversifying your tenant profile*: This involves owning properties at different rental income amounts so that you appeal to a wide sector of the market. For example, if you have a house as an investment and are charging, say, $800 per week in rent, then you might be better off investing in an apartment next at a rental level of $400 per week (to reduce the risk and financial impact of vacancy). Also, different types of properties will appeal to different markets – some will appeal more to couples and singles, for example, whereas others will be more suitable for professionals or for families. It is advantageous if all your properties do not appeal to any one market.

- *Investing in a different market to where your home is located:* While your home is purchased for different reasons than building wealth, investing in a different geographic location from your home is advisable. I'm not necessarily suggesting a different state, but a different suburb is advisable for the purposes of geographic diversification.

Land tax is insidious! Ignore it at your peril

As discussed earlier in this chapter, one of the hallmarks of investment-grade property is a strong land component. The consequence of this is that it can attract land tax. Land tax is payable if you own land (other than your home) that exceeds the tax-free threshold, which is different for each state in Australia (To find out the current threshold for your state, do an online search for 'land tax state revenue [insert your state]'.)

The tax-free thresholds are per individual so, from a pure land tax perspective, you and your spouse are better off owning one property each – if you own two properties, for example. Of course, structuring ownership solely to minimise land tax would be silly – because you need to weigh up many considerations and land tax is only one of them.

Indeed, your land tax liability is unlikely to be significant when you begin your investment journey. However, in time, with the power of compounding growth, your land tax liability may start to become costlier. Therefore, it is important to consider how to best manage this future liability when you first purchase the property – because you will have to live with the ownership structure for the whole ownership period. (Changing the ownership structure in the future is likely to be cost prohibitive because it triggers stamp duty and capital gains tax.)

Your choice of ownership structure is also complicated by the fact that most states charging a higher rate of land tax for property owned by a discretionary family trust. The following table illustrates the different land tax liabilities for land valued at $1 million when held in different states and via a trust or personal name. As you can see, the difference can be considerable – for example, the difference between trust and personal name ownership in NSW is nearly $9,000 p.a. in extra land tax. If you would like to hold an investment property in a trust, then doing so in Victoria is probably the best choice.

Annual land tax on $1m of land value:
Family trust versus personal name

	NSW	VIC	QLD
Personal name	$7,316	$2,975	$4,500
Trust	$16,000	$6,438	$12,500

The best way to minimise the impact of land tax is to spread your property assets across various ownership structures (for example, personal names, a trust and an SMSF) and across various states. Again, you should not structure investments purely based on projected land tax outcomes because land tax is only one of many important considerations. Consider all the factors and required attributes discussed in this chapter, with potential future land tax one factor among the others.

What about commercial property?

Often clients ask me whether they should invest in residential or commercial property. I typically advise clients to invest in residential property first. Then, when they have accumulated a significant asset base (net worth), they could consider investing in commercial property. Investors are often attracted to commercial property for its high-income yield. However, as discussed in Golden Rule #4, the most efficient way to build wealth is to do it in two steps – build your asset base first and then start investing for income. Residential property's primary role is to help you build your asset base.

Commercial property has a different risk profile than residential property because residential property is a necessity and, as such, the underlying demand for residential housing doesn't fluctuate very much. This means enough demand typically exists from tenants to ensure your vacancy risk remains low. However, commercial property is largely affected by the health of the domestic economy (determined by macro and micro economic factors). This means commercial property investors can expect higher amounts of volatility. For example, commercial property vacancy periods can be quite lengthy (so your commercial property might be vacant for, say, six months before you find a suitable tenant). As such, you need to have a relatively strong asset base to weather some of these storms.

The sub-$10 million commercial property market is also quite competitive because wealthy individuals and SMSFs can afford to invest in this sector of the market. This means that investment returns can be quite compressed (as multiple purchasers compete for the same property). Commercial properties in the $10 million to $50 million range often present as better opportunities because they're too large for wealthy individuals and too small for institutions. As such, this price range tends to be a bit of a sweet spot in the market. In my professional experience, the best way to access this sector of the market is through small unlisted property syndicates, which typically consist of around 20 investors who pool their capital together with some borrowings to invest in a commercial asset. Of course, these are very complex transactions and I strongly suggest that you do not invest without specialist professional advice.

Using other people's money to build your wealth

The great advantage of property is your ability to use other people's money – through borrowing – to leverage your returns. Let's look at an example to really illustrate this. Assume you buy a $500,000 property (excluding all costs) funded by an 80 per cent loan ($400,000) and 20 per cent cash deposit. The property costs you $1000 per month to hold (that is, rent minus expenses and interest = $1000). If you sell the property in 10 years for $1 million, to work out your pre-tax return on your cash you first need to work out how much cash you contributed towards the investment. You paid an initial deposit of $100,000 plus $12,000 p.a. for 10 years, which equals $220,000 in total. You made $500,000 profit, which, after taking out your total contribution, works out to be a compounding annual return of 15.7 per cent p.a. (on your cash). Now, if you were able to borrow the full cost of the property ($500,000) and only meet the holding costs from your own cash flow ($12,000 p.a.), your pre-tax cash return increases to 28.8 per cent p.a. – because while your return is the same (at $500,000), your cash contribution reduces to only $120,000. This is the power of using other people's money – that is, borrowing from the bank. The less cash you contribute towards an investment, the higher your cash return is.

But that is not to say that you should all go out and borrow as much as you can and buy any old property. Not at all. You will have a maximum borrowing capacity – which is the lower of:

- how much the banks will lend you

- how much you can afford to borrow without putting your present and future cash flow under pressure.

Borrowing capacity is a scarce resource and it should be allocated to achieve the highest return. For example, if my personal borrowing capacity is $1 million, I want to use that $1 million to buy the highest quality property or properties that I can find. Make sure your borrowings are working as hard as possible for you.

Sometimes people hold onto under-performing properties. They conclude they are not worth selling because 'they aren't costing me anything' – that is, the rental income pays for all expenses and interest. However, if these properties have loans against them, they are costing you something – the scarce asset of your borrowing capacity. That borrowing capacity might be better allocated towards a better property. It comes down to opportunity cost – that is, what are you missing out on by continuing to hold onto an under-performing property? I have always advised that there is never a bad time to buy an investment-grade property – and, equally, there's never a bad time to sell a non-investment-grade property.

Loan structuring

When it comes to structuring mortgages, seeking advice from an investment-savvy mortgage broker is very important, because how your loans are structured affects your cash flow, risk, tax and ability to build wealth. I have written a book (*Smart Borrowers Handbook*, in its second edition) which, of course, I highly recommend and which offers much more information in this area. The following sections summarise my seven loan structuring tips.

Always borrow the maximum and use an offset

The first thing to be very mindful of is that you only have one opportunity to crystallise the maximum tax-deductible loan in respect to a property – that is, when you first purchase it. You cannot contribute cash and borrow a lower amount when you purchase a property and then subsequently increase the loan later (because the purpose or use of the additional funds will determine whether the loans are tax-deductible or not). The second thing to keep in mind is that it is repeatedly demonstrated to me (through dealing with hundreds of clients) that one thing doesn't change in life and that is change itself. Therefore, you will do yourself a great service to structure your finances to give you as much flexibility as possible.

Let me explain using an example. Say Dr Smith purchases an investment property for $500,000. He has repaid his home loan and has no other debt. Dr Smith has $190,000 of cash savings to contribute to the investment. He has two options (ignoring costs for this example): he can borrow the $310,000 he needs ($500,000 minus $190,000 cash) or he can borrow the full $500,000[1] and deposit $190,000 in a linked offset account. The latter option won't cost him any more because the bank will only charge interest on the net balance of $310,000.

Dr Smith can still access the $190,000 cash savings at any time. There are no restrictions as the bank originally approved a loan facility for $500,000 and the balance in the offset has no impact on the loan balance – just the interest payable. For example, if a few years after purchasing the property Dr Smith decides to undertake some renovations to his home costing approximately

$100,000, he can withdraw this amount from the offset. Of course, because the balance in the offset has reduced, his interest bill will increase but all the interest will be tax-deductible. If he hadn't structured his loan with an offset, he would have had to borrow the $100,000 for the renovations and the interest on that loan would not have been tax-deductible. In summary, it is nearly always the best approach to borrow the full cost of a property and deposit cash in the offset.

Where economical, structure repayments as interest only

In keeping with the previous tip, this one also relates to preserving future tax benefits and maximising your flexibility. Structuring your loan repayments as interest only (and not principal and interest) provides the following benefits:

- It allows you to accumulate all surplus cash in the offset instead of reducing the loan principal. This preserves the loan principal at its original value, which might be important for future tax benefits (like the preceding strategy). This even might be appropriate for your home loan because your home may become an investment property one day.

- It reduces your financial commitment to the lowest level. The benefit of this is twofold. Firstly, it minimises your risk in case of a change of circumstances such as a temporary reduction in income. Secondly, it allows you to direct your surplus cash flow as you see fit from time to time. For example, an investment opportunity might arise that necessitates you to pay interest only on your home loan for a few months.

During 2017, banks increased interest rates applicable to loans with interest only repayments. Therefore, these products now attract an interest rate premium compared to principal and interest loans. In some circumstances, you might find this interest rate premium to be too costly and feel tempted to accept a principal and interest loan. However, you need to consider carefully the pros and cons discussed here. If you're at the beginning of your investment journey, remember that asset acquisition is a priority, not debt reduction. However, if you have already acquired the necessary investment assets, you should direct surplus cash into offsets to reduce debt.

Minimise security

Be careful not to give the bank too much security – a property's title is better held in your possession than the bank's. The general rule is to try to keep your loan to value ratio at or around 80 per cent of the security's value. This will still allow you to get the lowest rate while not giving the bank any more security than it needs.

A common example of 'giving the bank too much security' is where a client might have a small home loan for, say, $200,000. The client then purchases an investment property for $550,000 and borrows $580,000 to fund this purchase (including stamp duties). The bank will often hold the client's home and the new investment property as security. However, if the client's home is worth, say, more than $900,000, the bank doesn't need to also take the new investment property as security. The home by itself will provide plenty of security for the home and investment loan.

The advantages of holding onto the title are that you can take a clear title to another lender to get a new loan and your existing lender does not need to know anything about it. Also, selling a property without a mortgage (that is, clear title) is an easier process and you have full control over how to use the sale funds (whereas if the bank holds the title, it can force you to use all the funds to repay debt).

Diversify lenders

Putting all your eggs in one basket is rarely a prudent thing to do in many (if not all) areas in life, including dealing with banks. The advantages that come from diversifying lenders are many, including:

- Sometimes a lender knows too much about you and, therefore, has too much control over your personal, business and investment matters. Banks are good servants but bad masters.

- You can better manage (maximise) your borrowing capacity by using multiple lenders – of course, it's still important to borrow within your safe limits.

- Banks are less likely to get 'lazy' if they know they don't have all your business. This keeps them on their toes and prevents them from becoming complacent.

- Property valuations commonly vary significantly from one bank to the next. Having a relationship with two or more banks (or, better still, a mortgage broker) will allow you to maximise your borrowable equity (that is, how much you can borrow against a property).

- When considering fixed rates, you have more than one lender to choose from without needing to refinance.

Avoid cross-securitisation

This tip relates to the two preceding ones on minimising security and diversifying lenders. Cross-securitisation is where any one loan uses more than one property as security. A simple example of cross-securitisation is where you have an investment loan secured by two properties: your home and the investment property. Here are my top three reasons you must avoid cross-securitisation:

1. *It does not allow you to maximise borrowable equity because of a lack of control over valuations:* It is not by chance that this is my first reason for avoiding cross-securitisation. Maximising your borrowable equity is critically important because the sooner you invest, the more money you make over time (because of compounding capital growth). If you avoid cross-securitisation you can determine which properties to revalue and when. Revaluing all the properties you own at the same time is unlikely to make sense. This is because the amount and quality of recent sales of comparable properties often determine if it's advantageous to revalue a property or not. If few comparable sales are available, you should try to defer any bank valuations. If your loans are cross-securitised, the bank will want to revalue all the properties that secure your mortgages – not just the ones you want to revalue. Consequently, you might get a mix of higher and lower valuations that may negatively impact on your overall borrowable equity (with the lower valuations more than offsetting the value of the higher valuations).

2. *Tying you to a lender reduces your flexibility:* If all your mortgages are cross-secured, your banking can become very entangled and it may prevent you (or make it very costly and difficult) to take one property away from your existing bank to get a better deal. You may want to use a new lender because, for example, it's offering a special (fixed) rate or perhaps it has a higher borrowing capacity and you have fully utilised your existing bank's borrowing capacity. However, you may not want to refinance your whole portfolio. Having all your properties separately secured gives you more flexibility because you might be able to refinance one property to the new lender. This will probably help you maximise your borrowing capacity too (through increased borrowable equity).

3. *You have no control over sales proceeds:* If your mortgages are cross-secured, the bank can control all sales funds (if you sell a property) and force you to contribute them to repaying debts. However, if there is no cross-securitisation, the bank can only demand repayment of the mortgages secured by that property. It is then up to you what you do with the balance. This is important because you might be selling property to realise cash reserves – allowing the bank full control over your money negates the benefit of selling in the first place. This is an important risk management point because many investors rely on the assumption that if things go pear-shaped on an investment, they can sell and walk away with cash. This might not be possible if you are cross-securitised.

Never mix business with pleasure

Sometimes having your business (if you're self-employed) and private banking with the one bank might seem convenient. It could very well turn out to be very convenient and you may not run into any trouble. However, I have seen plenty of situations where this hasn't worked out well for clients. The problem with this is that the bank has too much control and it knows too much.

For example, if you have a dip in revenue for a few months and then apply for a personal investment loan, they might start asking questions. Instead, if you separate your business banking from your personal banking, you control the amount of information each side has. This might be less important when things are going well, but can become a lot more important if your financial situation becomes a little more complex or changes. In hindsight, it's rarely worthwhile to use the same bank for business and personal banking.

To a lesser extent, the same can be true for personal and invest-ment lending too. That is, consider using different lenders.

Stagger fixed rate expiry

Most investors will be long-term borrowers. They will typically have investment mortgages for most of their lives. In fact, it's good to come to terms with this – that is, holding a healthy level of good debt (tax-deductible debt) for most of your lifetime is important and efficient. As such, it makes sense from time to time to fix mortgage interest rates – and, when doing so, staggering the expiry of fixed rates is good interest rate management. For exam-ple, it might make more sense to have some of your mortgages on a variable rate, some fixed for three years and some fixed for five years. This gives you more flexibility to review your interest rate management (fixed versus variable) at regular intervals.

Avoiding tenant horror stories

Once they have selected their investment property and secured their loan structures, some prospective property investors become concerned about the implications of having nightmare tenants in their property. They are worried these tenants may cause damage, not pay their rent and/or be difficult to remove. While risks are present with every investment, in my personal and professional experience, tenant risk can easily be minimised. The following sections take you through some of the basics.

Securing the right property and right manager

If you select the right property, you're unlikely to have tenant issues. The right property will attract a high calibre tenant who tends to want to maintain a clean record (that is, no poor payment history and so on). Making sure you have a good, experienced property manager is also critical. An experienced property manager will know what signs and history to look for when selecting a low-risk tenant and undertake various background checks.

The horror stories that you read or hear about largely relate to properties in lower socio-economic areas, and to people who self-manage their investment property and/or have the wrong property manager in charge.

When it comes to property managers, you must spend a bit of time holding your property manager accountable. As with many things, the squeaky wheel gets the most oil. That's not to say that you should make a pain of yourself, but it is important to check in a couple times per year to ensure inspections have been completed and to ensure the property is being adequately maintained. If you look after your property well, your tenant likely will also.

When it comes to undertaking maintenance, in my experience, make sure you are being quoted a reasonable cost. Some tradespeople who work for property managers will over-quote in the hope that the landlord (you) will automatically approve the spend. Instead, instruct your property manager to get a couple of quotes – especially if the job involves a reasonable amount of money. I recommend spending about one to two hours per year in 'managing the manager' – it doesn't take up a lot of time, and it is important to do.

Not fearing tenant turnover

Some people think tenant turnover (that is, losing a tenant and having to replace them) is all bad. However, this is not always the case. Sometimes continually increasing the rent you charge a tenant is difficult – particularly if they have occupied the property for many years (say, more than five). In this situation, I commonly see property rented at below market rates. Therefore, one of the advantages of turning a tenant over is that you can advertise the property at a market level rent. That said, your preference in this area depends on what's most important to you – retaining a secure, long-term tenant who is looking after the property or maximising the property's income.

What is your debt exit strategy?

Do you need a debt exit strategy? The answer to this question largely depends on when you want to retire. That is, if your retirement is 15 or more years away, chances are you won't need to worry about a debt exit strategy because your loan to value ratio (the level of debt compared to value) at retirement will likely be relatively low – assuming your property is investment-grade. However, if you would like to retire within the next 15 years, you may need to develop a debt repayment strategy because continuing to hold a lot of debt in retirement is not advisable. If you do take debt into retirement, I recommend it should be less than 40 per cent of the asset's value – therefore, the rent will more than cover the property's expenses. However, you need to hold a property for a considerable time to achieve this (or be able to reduce debt).

If you do need to reduce debt, you can consider a couple of options. Firstly, you could sell a property. For example, you might purchase three investment properties with the view of selling one to reduce debt at retirement and retaining two for the long term. Secondly, you may use some of your superannuation to reduce debt.

Irrespective of what your strategy is, I would like to make two points:

1. You need to consider how much debt you are comfortable taking into retirement. You need to consider the impact of

your repayments when interest rates are 7, 8 or 9 per cent, for example.

2. If your strategy does include an asset sale, consider the impact of capital gains tax (CGT). For example, it might be advantageous for you to own the property within an SMSF because, if you then sell the property post retirement (when the SMSF is in pension phase), you will be able to avoid paying any CGT.

Golden Rule #7 summary

Throughout this chapter we have learnt:

- Investing in property all hinges on selecting the right asset. I cannot overstate how important it is to select the right property.

- Investment-grade property is defined as property that doubles in value every 7 to 12 years, on average, over the long term. Sub-categories of investment-grade property are possible, and the higher the quality, the higher the expected returns. Entry-level property, for example, will probably take 12 years to double in value.

- A property must possess three attributes to be considered investment-grade. Firstly, it must have a strong land value component – more than 50 per cent for apartments and 60 per cent for houses. Secondly, it must have scarcity – that is, an imbalance of supply and demand – with demand being considerably higher than supply. Land supply, location and architectural style are the main influences of scarcity. Thirdly, the property must have proven its ability to generate strong returns. You should be able to track a property's growth rate over the past two to three decades and see that it's investment-grade.

- Off-the-plan and new-build properties tend to not possess all three required attributes and, therefore, do not make good investments.

- Given that buying the right property is absolutely critical, obtaining advice from a reputable buyers' agent makes sense – even if it's a second opinion.

- Planning out your property portfolio allows you to diversify geographically, by tenant type and by price point. It also allows you to take steps to minimise expenses such as land tax.

- Growing wealth initially with residential property before branching out into commercial property is typically the better option.

- You must structure your loans so that you maximise your tax benefits, minimise your risk and maximise your borrowable equity. Doing so will help you accumulate a property portfolio quickly and painlessly .

- The right property plus the right managing agent equals fewer problems (and fewer tenant hassles).

- If you plan on carrying a large level of debt into retirement, you must plan your debt exit strategy.

---

1 Assuming that Dr Smith has equity in his home (for example) to assist in securing the $500,000 loan together with the investment property (also used as security).

PROTECT YOUR INVESTMENTS FROM EXPECTED AND UNEXPECTED RISKS

As the saying goes, you should 'plan for the worst and hope for the best'. Smart investing aims to achieve the highest return for the lowest risk, while the risk–return payoff suggests that if you want a higher return, you must accept more risk. Investing in a term deposit is very low (almost no) risk, for example, but the returns are lower too.

However, some of the world's greatest investors seek to turn the risk–return payoff on its head. They structure their investments in a way that means returns are high and risk is very low. For example, Warren Buffett invested $5 billion in Goldman Sachs at the height of the GFC (just after the collapse of Lehman Brothers). Buffett purchased preferred stock and options in Goldman Sachs when its share price was falling and demanded a 10 per cent dividend to protect his downside – that is, if the share price didn't recover for a long time, at least he'd still receive an income stream. The deal was so expensive for Goldman that they bought back the preference shares. In the end, Buffett made $3.1 billion from the deal.

The mantra when investing is 'always protect your downside risk'. Ask yourself, what could go wrong? This is exactly what you should do in other areas of your life too. You need to think about all the things that could go wrong and consider what you can do to minimise the risk. You should take four steps (in this order):

1. Identify actions you can take now to avoid or minimise the risk

2. Insure against the risk – which is essentially transferring the risk to someone else for a fee

3. Alter your strategy

4. Accept the risk.

This chapter discusses the most common risks that can compromise an investment strategy's success – including accident or illness, job loss, higher interest rates, getting sued and relationship breakdowns.

Insuring your most valuable asset

Without a doubt, most people's most valuable asset is their ability to earn an income. Depending on health, most people can work for approximately 45 years (from age 20 through to age 65). Assuming you can generate an average income of $80,000 per year from age 25, the pre-tax value of that 40-year income stream in today's dollars would be over $2 million[1]. I'm sure you agree that this is an extremely valuable asset. Of course, if you have the capacity to generate more income than $80,000 per year, the value increases further.

The interesting thing is that although the clear majority of people insure their car against loss or damage, significantly fewer people insure their income. If your uninsured car were destroyed, it might take you a couple of years to recover financially. However, compare this to losing your income for an extended period. Perhaps you would never fully recover financially from such a loss.

While we hope the likelihood of losing our ability to earn an income for an extended period is extremely low, the financial impact of it occurring is massive.

The predominant concern or risk is long-term incapacity. That is, if you broke your leg and couldn't work for eight weeks, financially, you would probably recover in a relatively short period of time – you hopefully have some savings, sick leave, annual leave and family to help. However, if you were involved in a car accident and couldn't work for the next seven years, it is very likely that such an event would put a big dent in your financial plans. Long-term incapacity has a severe financial impact – we don't need to be too concerned about short-term incapacity.

Most financial strategies are premised on the assumption that we can get out of bed in the morning and generate income. Put differently, financial strategies are dependent upon our ability to contribute a regular amount from income towards our investments. In the absence of these regular contributions, most financial strategies would fail. Therefore, this is a key and fundamental risk that must be considered.

Attitudes to insurance

Many people harbour negative attitudes towards insurance. Their main concern is that if they ever need to make a claim, the insurance company won't pay out, so they tend to see the cost of insurance as a waste of money. Indeed, recent Australian research by financial consultants Rice Warner suggests that the median income protection cover, on average, only meets 16 per cent of an individual's needs – that is, most Australians are significantly underinsured.

Some insurance advisors have also created the negative stigma associated with seeking insurance advice by overselling or over-recommending insurance cover. That is, some insurance advisors would recommend an amount of cover to maximise their commission income. To highlight this point, the federal government (via ASIC) completed research in 2017 into the practices of some insurance advisors – and I was astounded by the amount of insurance that some advisors recommended! The goal of this chapter is to cut through all the sale-spiels and demonstrate to you exactly what cover you need, how much to spend and how to structure it.

When it comes to insurance, coverage required is not a black-or-white answer. It's not a case of whether you should have some or nothing at all. Instead, it's really about the amount of cover that is appropriate for you. Therefore, if you feel you have a pretty low risk profile, chances are you still need some level of insurance cover, but maybe less than most.

Types of cover

Four predominant types of insurance products are relevant to investors, and I provide a summary explanation of each of these products in the following sections. Of course, the quality and cost of these products will vary between insurance providers so it's important to understand the detail (that is, get professional advice) before you arrange any policies.

Income protection

Income protection provides cover in case you cannot perform your usual occupation as a result of sickness or injury. Income protection policies generally pay a monthly benefit for a specific period of time – called the 'benefit period' – usually until age 65 (although cover inside super often only pays a two-year benefit; more about this later in the chapter). Importantly, income protection does not cover you for involuntary unemployment (such as loss of job or redundancy). The payment of an income protection benefit allows you to continue to afford to pay for living expenses and financial commitments, and you are able to insure up to 75 per cent of your gross income. (Providers restrict coverage to this level to provide a financial incentive for people to recover and return to work.)

Most income protection policies will have a 'waiting period', which is the length of time you need to be incapacitated for until you can claim a benefit. Waiting periods usually range from 30 days to 280 days – so this is an important aspect to check before signing up.

Insurers typically offer two types of insurance contracts: indemnity or agreed value. Indemnity contracts require you to prove the amount of income you were earning before you became incapacitated at the time of claiming a benefit. Agreed value contracts are financially underwritten when the insurance contract is established – and, therefore, you don't need to prove your income when you make a claim. I recommend agreed value contracts because at least you will get what you pay for. For example, if you have an agreed value contract that provides for a $10,000 per month benefit payment but your pre-disability income had gone to, say, $5000 per month, you will still receive the full $10,000. However, under an indemnity value contract, you would only receive a benefit of $5,000 per month – even though your past premiums may have been based on a much higher level of cover. Income protection insurance premiums are almost always tax-deductible.

Life insurance

Life insurance pays a lump sum benefit after death, and can also be used to provide for the welfare of any financial dependants in the event of your death. The lump sum benefit can be used to repay debt and replace the income that you would have otherwise contributed to your family (that is, it can contribute to covering living expenses). Life insurance can be owned by you personally or your super fund. If life insurance is owned personally, the premium is not tax-deductible. However, if life insurance is owned by your super fund, the fund will be entitled to a tax deduction for the premium (a 15 per cent tax deduction). Therefore, I typically recommend people hold life insurance inside super.

Total and permanent disability

Total and permanent disability (TPD) insurance will provide you with a lump sum benefit (payment) in the event that you suffer an illness or injury and so have no prospect of ever returning to work. An example of this would be a car accident victim who has become a quadriplegic. A TPD benefit can be used to repay debt, pay for medical and care expenses, make modifications to your home and so on.

TPD insurance is the least claimed product because it covers a narrow element of risk. If you are deemed totally and permanently disabled, you'll very likely also be able to make a claim on income protection insurance. Therefore, for most people, the required amount of TPD insurance will depend on the level of income protection insurance held. Like life insurance, the premium for TPD insurance is not tax-deductible if it's in your personal name but is tax-deductible if it's inside super. Again, typically, I recommend people hold TPD insurance inside super.[2]

Trauma/critical illness

Trauma or critical illness insurance provides a lump sum benefit *upon diagnosis* of a 'specified condition'. Most trauma insurance policies have a list of approximately 25 to 30 specified conditions. Statistically, a specified condition usually includes cancer or heart-related conditions (such as heart attack or heart surgery). Premiums for trauma insurance are not tax-deductible and you cannot put this cover inside super. Most people use trauma insurance to repay debt, cover out-of-pocket medical treatment expenses and voluntary time off work. For example, if I was diagnosed with cancer tomorrow, I could immediately claim a benefit on my trauma insurance contract. I could then use that money to, say, fly to Germany to obtain specialist chemotherapy treatment. I regard trauma insurance as the most 'optional' of all the four insurance products. The reality is that if I was diagnosed with cancer tomorrow, I would probably start treatment pretty quickly – probably within the next week. Given this, I would likely be able to claim on income protection insurance at this time (subject to my waiting period). Therefore, the amount of trauma insurance you might need greatly depends on the level of your income protection cover.

Selecting an insurance provider

When it comes to comparing and selecting insurance products the following three considerations need to be balanced:

1. The cost of cover (that is, the annual premium net of any tax deduction)

2. The quality of cover (more about this below)

3. The quantum of cover (the amount of benefit insured).

Two of the three considerations (cost and quantum) are self-explanatory. The quality of cover, however, is a very important consideration – arguably, the most important of the three. The quality of an insurance product essentially refers to a product's *depth* of cover. This means that if you need to make a benefit claim, a high-quality product will maximise your chances of having your claim approved by the insurer.

Perhaps this is best explained using an example. All income protection insurance policies will include a definition of what constitutes 'partial incapacity' (that is, if you are still able to work but not at 100 per cent). A very basic income protection product will typically have a one-tier definition (duties only – see the following list). However, a good quality income protection policy will have a three-tier definition. This means that you can prove that you are partially incapacitated by fulfilling any one (or all) of three tests, which typically include:

1. *Duties definition:* You can claim a benefit if you become unable to perform one or more income-earning duties due to sickness or injury.

2. *An hours work test:* You can claim a benefit if you are unable to work your usual hours. If you are unable to work more than 10 hours per week, an insurer will normally consider you totally incapacitated. However, if you are returning from injury or sickness, you might not be able to work a full week but might want a staged return to work where you work more than 10 hours per week. A good quality policy will provide for this.

3. *Loss of income test*: If, due to sickness or injury your income has dropped by 20 per cent or more, you can claim a benefit. This will suit people who are paid on commission or are self-employed. They might still be able to perform their duties and work 40 hours per week, for example, but their volume of work has diminished. Therefore, this test will be handy.

This is only one example of how the quality of a product influences its value. Of course, insurance products are complex and include many different clauses and tests. Therefore, it is important to get advice to ensure you know what you are paying for. The good thing is that, unlike with most other things in life, the better quality products are often the lower cost options, and you rarely need to pay more to get more when it comes to insurance. This is because insurance providers target certain occupations and clients and then price their products to attract the occupations they want – and repel the business they don't.

Level or stepped premium – a big decision?

Insurance companies usually offer two types of premiums: level or stepped. A stepped premium increases with age (because the older you are, the greater the chance of illness and therefore the higher risk you are). A level premium is calculated by averaging the stepped premium over the life of the contract and providing a discount. Therefore, level premiums tend to cost more in the earlier years but a lot less in the later years. Also, assuming you have the same amount of insurance with the same insurance provider for the whole term of the contract, the total costs of a level premium contract are less than total costs for a stepped contract.

Having said that, I'm not a huge fan of level premium contracts for the following reasons:

- They essentially lock you into having the same level of cover with the same provider until age 60 or beyond. The reason for this is that once you are more than 8 to 10 years into a level contract, you've typically already paid a lot more than what you would have under a stepped contract, and so you may as well retain the cover for the rest of the contract's life because you (sort of) have already pre-paid for future cover.

- As your asset position improves, you often need less insurance. When people begin investing and have high family commitments (in their thirties and forties), they have greater insurance needs. However, assuming they invest wisely, they probably need less insurance in their fifties and arguably none in their sixties (when all their income comes from investments). Level contracts, therefore, don't give you the flexibility to adjust the level of cover depending on your circumstances and financial evolution.

The sceptic in me says that level contracts were developed for the main benefit of insurance advisors and insurance companies – that is, to lock in a client (along with their revenues and commissions) for the long run. However, I acknowledge that they will suit some people.

If you are going to establish a level contract, think very carefully about it. A better solution may be a hybrid structure – part level and part stepped. For example, if you earn $20,000 per month, you may not want to insure for the maximum amount for the rest of your life. However, you also might not expect to ever have no income protection cover either – irrespective of your financial position. Therefore, maybe a core level of cover (say, for $7,000 per month) can be on a level premium and the rest on a stepped. This allows you to cancel or reduce the stepped portion as your financial position strengthens.

How much is enough?

As a general rule, I typically like to keep the total cost of insurance at less than 3 per cent of a client's gross family income. The cost can exceed this amount at times because it greatly depends on a client's risk tolerance and financial position – after all, it is just a general rule. If you are spending more than 3 per cent of your gross income on personal risk insurances, however, you need to pay close attention to it and review the cover each year to ensure it's still warranted and worthwhile.

Beware of 'cheap and easy' cover

We've all seen the TV commercials advertising cheap and easy life and income protection cover (often shown during the day or late at night). They suggest that you can ring up and arrange cover for a small weekly premium – no questions asked about medical history, no blood tests, no proof of income and so on. While this might seem to be a low-cost and easy way of establishing cover, however, these products are rarely worthwhile.

Firstly, the cover is typically not underwritten. Underwriting is the process the insurer goes through to understand the risk of ensuring a particular individual. The more thorough the under-writing process, the better the quality of cover – because when it comes to making a benefit claim, the insurer has less room to argue the claim is for a pre-existing condition. With no underwriting, the insurer also takes on more risk and, therefore, charges a higher premium. This means 'no questions asked' is not a positive when it comes to arranging insurance contracts.

Secondly, by comparison, products that are sold direct to consumers (such as via TV advertisements and online) are expensive. They might sometimes seem cheap but that's because the policies and coverage are very weak – for example, they are indemnity policies only, cover shorter benefit periods, have many exclusions and offsets, and no partial disability cover. In the main, they are just not worth getting.

If you are going to arrange insurance cover, always make sure you are getting what you're paying for.

Where to go to get your insurance cover

Providing advice in this area that will suit everyone is inherently difficult. Of course, everyone's situation is different and, as such, their approach to insurance might also need to be different. The following provides you a generic summary of how to structure insurances but please don't consider this as a substitute for personalised advice.

A possible way to structure your insurance is as follows:

- *Life and TPD insurance:* Industry super funds not only provide low-cost superannuation products but also offer insurance as an auxiliary product via group cover. Group cover means they aggregate the total amount of cover requested by their members and obtain an insurance contract for that amount. In theory, group cover should be cheaper than retail cover (but that's not always the case). For most people, obtaining life and TPD cover via an industry super fund is an adequate, simple and low-cost solution. To choose a fund, go to www.industrysuper.com. Be aware that premiums between various industry funds can vary dramatically so compare a couple of options (most have quoting calculators on their website).

- *Income protection insurance:* Income protection insurance is best owned in personal names – not inside super. The reason for this is that products inside super tend to be pretty basic (that is, they don't provide very deep cover). Given that I believe income protection is the most important insurance product, I also recommend not making any compromises. That said, arranging a split policy – where some cover is inside super and some is outside super – is possible. This means that your super fund will essentially pay for approximately 85 per cent of the premium, thereby having less impact on your personal cash flow. Again, income protection is by far the most important product to optimise. Therefore, I strongly advise you to seek advice from a reputable insurance advisor who will be able to provide personalised advice to help you balance out the three considerations of cost, quality and quantum of cover. Make sure the advisor is able to compare all risk and life insurers in Australia (there are 25 to 30) – some advisors only have a panel of one or two insurance providers, which doesn't offer enough choice. Refer to the final chapter in this book for more on how to select an advisor.

- *Trauma insurance:* Of all the four insurance products, I believe that trauma cover is the least important. Arguably, having very good quality income protection cover lessens the need for trauma insurance. That is not to suggest you should discount it, and it is still appropriate for some people – so long as they prioritise income protection, life and TPD insurance first. If you are interested in getting some trauma cover, speaking to a reputable insurance advisor is a good idea.

Tips to reduce the cost of cover

Insurance is relatively cheap when you are young. Not only are premiums low, but the amount of cover is substantial because you are many decades away from the contract end date – which is typically age 60 or 65. Obviously, as you get older, particularly in your forties and fifties, the cost of insurance begins to escalate, and it might become important to look for ways to reduce this cost. Reducing cover is often a better response than cancelling cover in totality. Here are a few tips:

- With respect to income protection insurance, the premium for a 90-day waiting period can often be half the cost of a premium with a 30- or 60-day wait period. Therefore, if your income protection insurance is costing too much, increasing the wait period might be a good way of reducing the cost of cover.

- Having some cover is better than none at all, so another way to reduce the cost of insurance is by reducing the benefit amount. Insuring your full income, for example, is not always economical or appropriate. Therefore, some compromises need to be made in order to achieve a more sustainable cost of cover.

- An easy way to reduce the cost of cover is to ensure your insurances are structured in a way that maximise your tax deductions. In summary, as covered earlier in this chapter, this means having life and TPD insurance inside super and holding income protection insurance outside super (in your personal name).

- Seek advice from a reputable, non-aligned advisor – that is, one who is not owned by a bank or insurance company. A non-aligned advisor should be able to compare all risk insurance providers in Australia and identify the most appropriate provider for you, at the best price.

Protecting yourself from other risks

As already mentioned, income protection does not provide cover in the case of involuntary unemployment. So how do you cover yourself if you lose your job? And what about other risks such as rising interest rates or getting sued. The following sections cover protecting yourself from these other risks.

What if you lose your job?

Because income protection insurance provides a benefit if you become sick or injured, not if you lose your job, you can't do much to protect yourself against the risk of job loss. (Other than the obvious – that is, becoming a valuable employee. As the saying goes, 'If you want more value, become more valuable'.)

One option is to take out loan repayment insurance. This type of insurance will usually cover your loan repayments for a period of time (usually six months) if you lose your job. For most people, this cover is not worthwhile. The role of insurance is to cover unknown and unexpected risks. Arguably, job security can be pro-actively managed by you to reduce your risk.

Rising interest rates

If your investment strategy includes borrowing money to invest, you need to ascertain your cash flow's sensitivity to interest rate movements. You need to ask yourself: what is the impact on your cash flow if interest rates increase by 2 per cent p.a.? If the projected impact is painful, you must proactively manage your interest rate exposure using fixed rates and accumulating buffers (cash and loan credit limits). It might not be necessary to fix all your debt (in fact, that is probably unwise) but fixing a proportion of your total debt over various fixed rate periods (I typically advise using a combination of 3- and 5-year fixed periods) is a prudent thing to do. Stagger the fixed rate maturity periods too – so all your fixed rates don't expire at the same time.

What if you get sued?

Some people are concerned about asset protection in the case of getting sued. While the prospect of being sued might be scary at first, looking closely often reveals the risk isn't as significant as first thought. An action is likely to result from two main areas:

- *Risk as a result of your employment*: Professional indemnity cover in Australia is very deep and very few examples exist of a person suffering personal loss as a result of an action. Essentially, for this to be a risk, you would have to be criminally negligent in performing your professional duties. There are, however, two other possible risks. The first one is trading while insolvent. A company director can be held personally liable if they are trading while insolvent. If you are self-employed, this is something to be mindful of. If you are a director of an Australian subsidiary company and the company is reliant upon the financial resources from its global parent, then make reasonable enquiries. Secondly, the other risk is maintaining a safe workplace. A director of a company may be held personally liable if they have been negligent in maintaining a safe workplace. This may be a concern (potential risk) for anyone who is self-employed in a business that is susceptible to workplace injuries.

- *Investment property tenant*: If a tenant (or visitor) injures themselves in your property, you may be held personally liable. Therefore, it is important to maintain good landlord cover, which will include some public liability cover. (Landlord insurance is usually pretty straightforward but, as always, check with your insurance broker if you have any questions.)

The preceding list is generic and, of course, may not apply to everyone. Therefore, if you have specific concerns, speak to your financial and legal advisors.

Estate planning matters

I meet a lot of new prospective clients who either do not have a will or have one that is outdated. I hope that having a will is not urgent, but it is important!

Drafting a will is important for anyone and if you have a reasonable amount of wealth, a blended family, have been divorced, care for someone with special needs and/or children, then I recommend you engage the services of an experienced lawyer. They will ask you all the right questions to uncover if you have any specific issues. If you have few assets and no dependants, using an online will provider is probably sufficient, (for example, Cleardocs, a Thomson Reuters company that works with Australian law firm Maddocks, is a reputable online provider that can provide wills – go to www.cleardocs.com/products-clearwill-online.html).

A testamentary trust is often an important feature of a will. Essentially, a testamentary trust is a trust that is created upon death and your assets are then held in that trust for your beneficiaries. This can substantially enhance asset protection and future tax minimisation. You should speak to your estate lawyer and financial advisor to ascertain if a testamentary trust is appropriate for your circumstances.

You should review your will every two to three years to consider if it is still appropriate. Are your executors still willing and able to look after your affairs? Do you have any 'at-risk' beneficiaries? (An 'at-risk' beneficiary is one who has a high risk of suffering personal loss, such as being successfully sued or going through a relationship breakdown.) Does your executor/s have the necessary information about your financial affairs? Have your wishes changed?

I recommend adults of all ages have an enduring power of attorney. A power of attorney allows someone you trust (your spouse, parent or adult child) to act as your agent – that is, to make personal and/or financial decisions on your behalf. Practically, this might involve signing documents if you are overseas or making decisions if you are injured. You might hold separate legal and medical powers of attorneys. It is important to speak to your estate lawyer about this.

Superannuation does not fall within the ambit of your will. Instead, the trustee of your super fund must decide where to pay your superannuation savings in the event of your death. Most super funds allow members to complete a death benefit nomination – which is your direction to them in respect of where to pay your super. These typically must be updated every three years. Some nominations are binding or non-binding – binding means the trustee is bound to follow your direction. Make sure your superannuation death benefit nominations are up to date (less than three years old).

Relationship breakdowns

A relationship breakdown can be costly, both emotionally and financially, but you can take steps to protect yourself. Seeking legal advice from an experienced lawyer in this regard is imperative; however, some important considerations include:

• If you cohabit with a partner for more than six months you may be considered to be in a de facto relationship by law. This depends on many factors – in particular, how you manage your finances (separately or together). However, if you begin cohabitating with your partner, consider arranging a binding financial agreement to protect yourself. Importantly, you also do not have to be cohabitating to be considered de facto – so if in doubt, seek advice.

- A pre-nuptial agreement deals with how property is to be split (and spousal maintenance paid) in the event of a relationship breakdown or divorce. They are usually entered into prior to marriage but can be entered into at any time. It is important that each party seeks independent legal advice prior to entering into a pre-nuptial agreement.

Golden Rule #8 summary

Here is a summary of the key points addressed in this chapter:

- Your ability to earn an income in the future is your most valuable asset. Most investment strategies are premised on the assumption that you will be able to continue to work – meaning, without your income, the investment strategy would fail. Therefore, you need to mitigate the risk that you are unable to work for an extended period of time (say more than 6 to 12 months).

- The most common four personal risk insurance products (in order of importance) are income protection, life, TPD and trauma cover.

- When selecting cover (especially for income protection) you must consider the quality of the policy – that is, how comprehensive the cover is.

- I prefer to maintain the total cost of all risk insurance to 3 per cent or less of gross family income.

- Stepped premiums provide more flexibility than level.

- Obtaining life and TPD insurance from an industry super fund is the better option, while income protection and trauma cover should be provided via a non-aligned advisor.

- Some options are available for reducing and managing the cost of cover.

- You can't do a lot to protect yourself against the risk of losing your job – so you need to proactively manage this risk as much as you can yourself within your job.

- You need to consider how sensitive your cash flow is to changes in interest rates. If it is sensitive, use fixed rates.

- If you are a director of a company, trading while insolvent and not maintaining a safe workplace are your two main potential risks.

- Make sure you have an up-to-date will and power of attorney, and review your will every two to three years. Consider whether a testamentary trust is appropriate.

- Consider protecting yourself against financial loss from a relationship breakdown using cohabitation agreements and/or pre-nuptial agreements.

---

1   This figure represents the present value of $80,000 p.a. for 40 years – that is, accounting for the impact of inflation.

2   Note that two types of definitions are possible with TPD cover: own-occupation and any-occupation. Own-occupation provides a higher level of cover and should not be held inside super. Any-occupation is suitable for most people (especially if they have good income protection cover) but seek professional advice to further explore the differences.

SELECTING A FINANCIAL ADVISOR YOU CAN TRUST

I've devoted this final chapter to finding a trustworthy financial advisor you can work with to achieve your investment goals – so please read this chapter even if you think all financial advisors are crooks and you have decided to never trust one.

Quality, professional advice can be invaluable. It can save or make you literally hundreds of thousands (or millions) of dollars. It can change your life. With this in mind, the million-dollar question is, 'How do you find an advisor that you can trust and is able to give you advice that will make you money?' The aim of this chapter is to give you the tools for finding and selecting such an advisor.

Of course, I am not impartial. As a financial advisor myself, I probably have (conscious and unconscious) biases. But let me reassure you that I don't view the industry through rose-coloured glasses. In fact, the reverse!

Nothing pisses me off more than hearing about poor unsuspecting people getting ripped off by a greedy financial advisor! My distaste for these situations is what has driven me to build my own advisory practice – to provide a trustworthy alternative. My view on the financial advice industry (practitioners and industry bodies alike) is that they have done very little over the past three decades to improve the quality of advice offered, preserve or improve the industry's reputation, and avoid people getting ripped off. Of course, a small number of advisors are doing a wonderful job.

A commission-based industry attracts self-serving individuals (not everyone, but some) so it needs tighter controls. Over the past 30 years, the industry could have been a lot more proactive. Overall, I have a pretty negative view of the industry and believe that 'good' financial advisors are in the minority. I wanted to share my views with you so that you know my biases lean towards the negative rather than positive. My goal with this chapter is not to convince you that all financial advisors are great. My goal is to give you the tools and knowledge so that you can find a good advisor you can trust.

One simple rule to avoid almost all financial advisor horror stories

We have all read the horror stories in the newspapers or seen them on television: Mum and Dad put their trust in a financial advisor. The advisor 'sells' them an investment that paid him a substantial commission. The investment was poor quality. Mum and Dad subsequently lose their life savings and the advisor goes unpunished. A new story like this comes up every few months. It's frightening and very upsetting!

I propose you can only do one thing to eliminate 99.9 per cent of all these stories occurring: remove all and any conflicts of interest. Once all conflicts of interest have been removed, working out if you should and can trust a particular advisor becomes a lot easier. In that situation, it simply comes down to whether the advisor has enough experience, knows what they are talking about and has a track record of producing good results.

Let me put it this way, would you be comfortable if your doctor (GP) was employed by a pharmaceutical company? Absolutely not! And that is why laws in Australia prevent pharmaceutical companies from owning and operating medical practices. I believe that we should have similar laws in the financial services industry (but I suspect the banks' political lobbying power will prevent this from happening). How do you choose which GP you visit? You make an assessment of whether the doctor knows what they are talking about, the results they produce and whether you feel comfortable dealing with them.

Therefore, before concluding that all financial advisors are crooks, I invite you to recognise that two types of financial advisors exist: independent advisors and conflicted advisors. When you read the next horror story in the newspaper ask yourself whether the advisor was independent or conflicted. I've no doubt you'll find they are always conflicted.

The rule here is that you should always avoid conflicted advisors. You should never, ever take financial advice from someone who has a conflict of interest. Doing so would expose you to significant risk – and it's just not worth it!

What is an independent advisor? Five important tests

To be truly independent I believe the advisor needs to satisfy five conditions:

1. *Take no commissions, referral fees or kickbacks:* The advisor should not accept any investment commissions, referral fees or any incentives for recommending any particular investment/s. This ensures they are impartial and have no personal stake in the advice outcome. They shouldn't make any more or less money (fees/revenue) based on their recommendations – irrespective of whether they recommend you invest in property, shares, super or nothing at all!

2. *Offer fixed fees:* They should not charge you a percentage fee on your investments because this creates a conflict too.

Independent advisors should charge you a fixed monthly, quarterly or annual fee for their service (or an hourly rate is fine too).

3. *Have nothing to sell you:* The advisor's business shouldn't make money from selling investments. For example, some financial planning businesses operate their own managed funds – that is not good. Some businesses will have relationships with property developers and receive commissions from recommending properties to their clients – this is definitely not good and you need to steer well clear! Some financial advisory practices offer the services of a buyers' agent – so if they recommend you invest in property, the buyers' agent can help you buy the right property for a fee. This, of course, creates a conflict of interest. This arrangement might not be a deal killer (and I know of at least one business that does this ethically), but beware that it is higher risk. The best case is that the advisor's business has nothing to sell you. They don't operate their own managed funds (shares), recommend direct shares (like a stock broker) or buy/recommend specific properties (through a buyers' agent). And they definitely have no links with property developers!

4. *Be privately owned with an AFSL and with no links to banks or investment providers:* All financial advisory businesses must have an Australian Financial Services Licence (ASFL) by law (or be authorised by an AFSL holder). The AFSL holder can direct advisors on which products/investments they can and cannot discuss and recommend. Therefore, it is important that the licence owner is an independent and privately-owned business. If the AFSL owner is a bank, for example, the advisor might only be allowed to sell bank-owned products (or have a very narrow list of other products).

5. *Demonstrate deep knowledge of all asset classes (especially property and shares)*: It is important that an advisor has a robust understanding of how to invest successfully using any and all asset classes. The main asset classes in Australia are residential and commercial property, shares/equities, bonds and cash. However, some financial planners know very little about investing in residential property. So how can they sit in front of their clients and recommend they invest in shares? My view is that they should know both property and shares equally well to be able to reach a reliable conclusion. If you walk into a Ford dealership, they will sell you a Ford. If you walk into a Holden dealership, they will sell you a Holden. If you visit an independent dealership, they'll likely know Ford and Holden cars equally well and, therefore, be able to recommend which one suits your circumstances best. To deliver independent, reliable advice with high integrity you must have a thorough understanding of all asset classes.

Understanding the lay of the land

The big four Australian banks plus AMP own or control close to 70 to 80 per cent of the financial advice and investment market. The banks own many different brands – so it's not always obvious that you're dealing with a bank-owned firm. In fact, 2017 research from Roy Morgan reveals that 'many consumers view institutionally-owned advice groups with different branding to their parent company as independent.' The same research also suggests that 74.9 per cent of advisors across all major financial planning groups sell their own products!

Often, a quick Google search should reveal whether the business is independently owned or not.

Alarmingly, over the past 10 years a new type of business has emerged where operators hold themselves out as financial advisory businesses. They advertise that they offer financial advice but, in reality, they have links with property developers and nearly always recommend clients to invest in said properties (which generate huge commissions). My advice is to steer well clear of these businesses. They are not advisory businesses. They are property marketing businesses! Again, a quick Google search or reading the fine print on these 'advisory' business's websites should reveal whether they are independent or not.

Independent financial advice practices are nearly always small businesses employing fewer than five people – or often fewer. These are typically the best businesses to deal with because the business's ethics and values are the 'alter ego' of the owner's. That is, the owner/founder has strong personal values about what is right and wrong, and the business is built around these values. A large business often doesn't exhibit these characteristics – its focus becomes less about right and wrong and more about maximising shareholder value.

Focusing on independent advisors

As far as I am concerned, the two types of advisors are independent and not independent. Many (but not all) non-independent (conflicted, commission-based) advisors have tarnished the industry's reputation and destroyed the public's impression of the value of financial advice.

For the rest of this chapter, my commentary only relates to reputable and independent financial advisors – advisors who are highly skilled and operate with the highest ethics and morals. Unfortunately, while they continue to be rare (but growing in number), these are the only advisors worth discussing.

The value in financial advice

Quality professional advice always pays for itself – a good lawyer, for example, will help you reduce risk or save money. An astute accountant will help you minimise the tax you pay. A reputable financial planner will make your money work hard for you. Assuming the professional advice is of a high standard, the value received should be (and typically is) always more than the price paid.

However, when it comes to financial advice, I'd like to suggest that many people confuse the *price* of financial advice with its *cost*. In most situations, cost is a lot more significant than the simple price (that is, the fee you pay). Let me explain:

1. *The price of financial advice:* The price of financial advice is simple to ascertain – it's the fee you pay your advisor. A point to stress again here is, as Warren Buffett says, 'Price is what you pay; value is what you get.'

2. *The cost of financial advice:* The cost of financial advice is reflected in things like missed investment returns, time wasted, money lost, stress, sleep lost, frustration and reduced happiness and satisfaction. These costs can be both financial and emotional. In the worst situations, the cost ruins people's lives.

Trying to work your investment strategy out all by yourself might reduce the price you pay to zero but arguably dramatically increases the cost.

Financial advice will always have a cost associated with it – irrespective of whether you use a financial advisor or not. You either chose to engage the services of a financial advisor or you become one yourself – that is, you become your own advisor. If you become your own advisor, you won't have to pay any fees – so that's a saving. However, you need to consider the impact on cost if you try to do it all yourself. What are the chances of you making a mistake and how much will that mistake cost? How much time will implementing and monitoring your strategy take you? Will the responsibility for working this all out yourself cause you stress?

Even if receiving independent advice helps you avoid just one or two mistakes, the value of this will likely more than pay for most advisors' fees. Having the ability to call upon the experience of a trusted professional to assist in making major financial decisions will surely reduce your stress too.

Therefore, it is important to consider both the price and cost of financial advice. The cost of trying to do it all yourself will often be more than the price of outsourcing it.

You should be better off, net of fees

Have a think about what your net worth might be in 10 or 20 years if you go it alone (with no financial advisor) – allowing for a few mistakes and delays along the way. Then consider the financial impact on your net worth if you eliminate these mistakes, time delays and earn a better investment return. If people honestly compare those two figures it will be obvious that you are better off receiving quality, independent financial advice, net of fees. Therefore, over time, the price of quality financial advice will be nil as the benefits gained more than outweigh the cost – because, for most people, the stakes are high.

The truth about independent advisors

Of course, independent advisors will not work for free. Any highly skilled, experienced professional wants to be fairly remunerated for their time, value and effort. Independent financial advisors are no different.

The challenge facing independent financial advisory businesses is how to scale the business (that is, to increase the size of the business in terms of revenue and clients while maintaining or improving the business's profitability) without watering down the value of advice. Owners can scale an independent financial advisory business in one of two ways:

1. Employ less-experienced advisors (because they cost less to employ)

2. Template (systemise) their advice.

To any proud and ethical independent financial advisor, neither of these options will be appealing. Quality financial advice is not templated – it's 100 per cent tailored.

Therefore, independent financial advisory businesses are inherently difficult (if not impossible) to scale. As such, most advisors max out at 150 client relationships because looking after more than 150 clients is very difficult. Therefore, an advisor needs to charge each client in the range of $3,000 to $5,000 per annum to build a decent business. This means that independent financial advisors need to target and attract people with a reasonable amount of complexity in their investments to justify this fee level.

I share this insight with you because I think it's important for you to understand how independent financial advisory businesses work. Quality, honest and independent advice is not cheap to deliver. In fact, it's expensive.

The massive chasm for us both to cross

ING Direct research from 2016 concluded that gen X and gen Y customers expect to pay a maximum of $250 for comprehensive face-to-face financial advice. This is tantamount to expecting to buy a brand-new Porsche for $5000! It's never going to happen.

Clearly, we both – that is, both sides of the advisor–client relationship – have a bit of work to do. Independent financial advisors need to better articulate the value of financial advice. And the public needs to recognise the two types of advisors and that only one is worth paying for – and that quality financial advice is incredibly valuable and worth a lot more than $250.

It's not opinion shopping – you want proof

Many people have the misconception that selecting and trusting a financial advisor involves opinion shopping – that is, you need to trust that an advisor's *opinion* is correct.

The good news is that this is completely incorrect. Financial advice can often be proven using simple maths and logic. It is really that simple. You don't need to trust an advisor's opinion – just ask them to use simple maths to demonstrate or explain to you why their strategy will work. If they can't do this, perhaps they don't have a robust and reliable methodology.

I am a very strong believer in using evidence-based methodologies. My clients don't pay me to speculate with their money, gaze into a crystal ball or invest in gut feelings or opinions. My clients only want to invest in 'sure things'. My clients want to enjoy the highest possible returns for the lowest possible risk. The only reliable way to achieve this is to use evidence-based strategies. These are strategies and methodologies that are rooted in academia, underpinned by sound fundamentals and have a strong track record. Of course, some risk is always present with investing. No guarantees exist. But you can certainly reduce your risk through adopting a sound, low-risk and proven methodology – like the eight golden rules discussed in this book.

Therefore, when seeking financial advice, you don't have to 'buy' an opinion. What you need to look for is an advisor who uses evidenced-based strategies.

You're paying for experience, not knowledge

Malcolm Gladwell popularised the '10,000-Hour Rule' in his best-selling book *Outliers*. The hypothesis is that anyone can become an expert in their field – all they need to do is 10,000 hours of practice.

When you engage an independent financial advisor, you are paying for two things: education (knowledge) and experience. Knowledge without experience is very dangerous, because experience shows us how best to apply the knowledge that we have acquired.

The internet has made an extraordinary amount of knowledge available to anyone with a computer. If you have the time and patience, you can replicate the knowledge of some of the top financial planners in Australia. However, their experience is much harder to replicate – the experience gained through spending circa 2000 hours per year advising hundreds of clients in different situations, year after year. Observing the results and outcomes of different decisions and approaches after 10, 15 and 20 years provides an advisor with invaluable experience. It would be reckless to undervalue how important this experience is.

Don't get emotional

We often get emotional about our money. Emotional financial decisions are usually influenced by fear or greed – and neither is very helpful when it comes to money. Fear will cause you to over-accentuate risks (and not see ways of managing risk) and become anxious and nervous. Greed may blind your ability to see (and appreciate) risk. The challenge with emotions is that often they unknowingly influence our decision-making at an unconscious level too.

Sometimes we see what we want to see. Why does the sun appear larger when it's close to the horizon (at sunrise or sunset) and comparatively smaller when it's above us (midday)? It's an optical illusion. Our eyes (and brain) lie to us, making us believe something we don't see. That's why when you take a photo of the sunset, you will see the truth – the sun looks smaller in the photo. The same happens with financial decisions when we are emotionally invested. We are either over-pessimistic or over-optimistic. Rarely are we balanced. Emotions cloud our judgment and stop us seeing the wood from the trees. We can become so focused on the problem that we cannot see the solution.

An independent financial advisor can help you make financial decisions without the influence of emotions. This can be incredibly valuable, especially in very stressful situations.

It's your responsibility! You cannot delegate it

You're investing your money and you must assume that no-one will look after it as well as you will. That is not to say that you should never fully trust anyone. However, it is your responsibility to do two things:

1. *You must understand money.* You must understand how investing works (that is, understanding the eight golden rules in this book). You don't have to become an expert, but you do need an understanding of the basic principles.

2. *You must understand what you are investing in.* Again, a basic understanding is fine. And if you don't understand, do not invest.

If you follow these two rules, any advisor or salesperson will find ripping you off very difficult.

Selecting a financial advisor you can trust summary

Hopefully this chapter has given you some insight into the financial advisory industry. In summary I have tried to make the following key points:

- Conflicts of interest are the cause of poor financial advice. Only deal with independent financial advisors.

- An advisor must fulfil five tests to be considered an independent financial advisor:

  1. Not accept any commission, kickback or referral fees in relation to investments

  2. Charge a fixed fee – no percentage fees

  3. Have nothing to sell you – no property, managed funds, shares or the like

  4. Be, or be authorised by, a privately owned financial advice licence holder – that is, no links with banks

  5. Have a deep understanding of all asset classes, including property and shares.

- The fees you pay a financial advisor are dwarfed by the potential cost of said advice. The cost of financial advice is reflected in things like missed investment returns, time wasted, money lost, stress, sleep lost, frustration, and reduced happiness and satisfaction.

- In order to manage (and perhaps reduce) the potential cost of financial advice, I suggest you only deal with an independent financial advisor, make sure that advisor uses evidence-based strategies and ensure your advisor has the level of experience that is appropriate for your situation and the complexity of your investment strategy.

- Most people tend to get emotional about their finances, which is why it's even more important to seek independent advice.

WRAP UP AND WHAT'S NEXT?

I hope this book has given you a much better understanding of how the game of successfully building wealth works. Now that you understand the rules of the game, you should have the confidence to develop your plan and start implementing it.

As Tony Robbins says, 'complexity is the enemy of execution' so my advice is to not overthink things too much. Keep your financial affairs as simple as possible. If you feel like everything's getting too difficult to understand, or you're getting confused with all the options available to you or receiving conflicting advice, just return to the simple eight rules contained in my book. The rules are simple to understand and simple to apply – don't let yourself get bamboozled by salespeople, marketing materials and media hype. The rules will reveal what you should do next.

Remember, you don't have to do all the work by yourself. Now that you know the eight rules to building wealth, you are well prepared to ensure that no-one can deceive you with self-serving advice or recommendations. Therefore, seeking advice from an independent financial planner is a less risky prospect than it was before reading my book – in fact, I would say low risk. Having the sole responsibility for formulating and implementing your family's financial plans can be very stressful. Letting advisors in to help you with this journey along the way is perfectly okay.

The pace of change these days is ever increasing. However, the eight rules outlined in my book almost certainly won't change –

because they are rooted in sound fundamentals and fundamentals rarely change. However, other aspects that I have discussed in this book will definitely change – things like passive managed fund providers, tax law and cash flow management tools. Therefore, if you would like to be kept up to date with these changes, I suggest you subscribe to my weekly blog (you can do this at www. investopoly.com.au) and/or my podcast (search for 'investopoly' in Apple's podcast app).

Again, if you have enjoyed this book, I would love it if you were generous enough to write a review online (on Amazon or Google). Doing so will help more people find this book and hopefully it will help them as it has helped you.

Finally, I wish you all the best with your investing. Building wealth is simple. Humans tend to make it more difficult than it needs to be. Stick with it, follow the eight rules and remember the following quote from Warren Buffett (which I have mentioned previously but it's so important):

> *Successful investing takes time, discipline and patience. No matter how great the talent or effort, some things just take time: You can't produce a baby in one month by getting nine women pregnant.*

INDEX

Notes

Notes

www.ingramcontent.com/pod-product-compliance
Lightning Source LLC
Chambersburg PA
CBHW031927190326
41519CB00007B/439